FREEDOM OF SPEECH

Issues and Cases

STUDIES IN
Speech

Consulting Editor

DON GEIGER

UNIVERSITY OF CALIFORNIA, BERKELEY

FREEDOM

OF

SPEECH

Issues and Cases

❦

Franklyn S. Haiman

NORTHWESTERN UNIVERSITY

Random House • New York

Congress shall make no law . . . abridging the freedom of speech . . . or the right of the people peaceably to assemble and to petition the Government for a redress of grievances.

First Amendment to the United States Constitution

No State shall make or enforce any law which shall abridge the privileges or immunities of citizens of the United States; nor shall any State deprive any person of life, liberty, or property, without due process of law. . . .

Fourteenth Amendment to the United States Constitution

Preface

Myth has it that plots for social change, particularly those involving libertarian doctrine, are hatched in the dark of night by groups of men huddled in animated discussion around coffee house tables. It must have been some such fantasy which influenced me and a gathering of my colleagues, all university teachers of speech, as we sat talking together one evening in 1960 in a coffee house in St. Louis' Gaslight Square, after a day of convention sessions of the Speech Association of America. For out of that discussion grew the conviction among us that teachers of speech ought to play a leading role in the scholarly study of problems of freedom of speech and in communicating an understanding of such problems to our students. Thus was planted the seed of what was to become the Committee on Freedom of Speech of the Speech Association of America, dedicated to the development of such leadership. It was as chairman of that committee that I was asked by Don Geiger and the editors at Random House to do this book, devoted to the same purpose. It is a nice historical accident that one of those who "hatched the plot" some fifty years earlier that had given birth to the Speech Association of America itself, Professor James M. O'Neill, was the man who first acquainted me with the American Civil Liberties Union and thus sparked my special interest in freedom of speech.

To my colleagues of the S.A.A. Committee on Freedom of Speech, particularly Alvin Goldberg of the University of Denver, Mark Klyn of the University of Washington, and Robert O'Neil of the University of California School of Law, I am indebted for the vigorous interaction that has sustained and nourished this interest, and more specifically for their invaluable critiques of this manuscript. To my associates in the Illinois Division of the American Civil Liberties Union, in particular William Brackett, John Coons, Nancy McDermid, Alexander Polikoff, George Pontikes, Joel Sprayregen, and Bernard Weisberg, I am indebted for the exposure they have provided me to brilliant legal minds working with clarity and eloquence on knotty First Amendment problems.

I have, of course, been heavily influenced and directed in my thinking by the incisive logic and persuasive discourse of many of the famous writers whose works are included in this volume. And finally, I owe a special debt of gratitude for my enthusiasm for the subject to countless hours of exhilarating discussion over the years with my former student, former Executive Director of the Illinois A.C.L.U., and cherished friend, John McKnight.

F.S.H.

Evanston, Illinois

Contents

Introduction

At no time in the history of the United States have more diverse voices clamored for public attention and competed for acceptance than those on the contemporary American scene. And at no time has so much argument been generated over the right of controversialists to speak.

Almost each new day brings with it a conflict in some part of the country involving demonstrations for racial equality—the picketing of a school board, a public rally, sit-ins, kneel-ins, wade-ins. The race supremacists, too, have been busy—holding meetings, campaigning for public office, distributing hate literature. A Communist speaker appears at one college, is prohibited at another. Anticommunist crusades fill their auditoriums with supporters, their coffers with money, and their radio programs with fervent fear appeals. A professor at a state university loses his job for condoning premarital sexual intercourse, while another on the same campus rides out a storm of protest over his article in the John Birch Society journal suggesting that President Kennedy was assassinated because he had decided to stop working for the Communist conspiracy. Courts in Pennsylvania and Georgia strike down local acts of movie censorship; "irreverent" language in *Who's Afraid of Virginia Woolf?* is banned in Boston; *Inherit the Wind* is barred from a high school stage in Illinois; and a comedian who liberally uses four-letter words to attack moral hypocrisy is arrested for obscenity in the nation's three largest cities.

There was an era when the struggle for freedom of expression was primarily a contest between political or religious dissenters and the governing authorities of church and state. But as democratic processes have become more prevalent, nonconformists have discovered that the people themselves can be as restrictive as their former rulers. As early as 1858, John Stuart Mill in his essay "On Liberty" dealt at length with the problems of a tyranny of the majority, and as recently as 1963 a leading American constitutional scholar has examined the contemporary manifestations of this same issue.[1] If we rely on the majority of our fellow citizens to understand and defend the freedom of speech clause of the First Amendment, we may be sorely disappointed. Although in 1960 the American Civil Liberties Union, dedicated to that purpose, could announce a doubling of its ranks during the decade just ended, its total membership was still only sixty thousand. At the same time, the Purdue Opinion Poll was reporting that among high school students across the nation—who presumably reflected to some degree parental attitudes as well —60 per cent believed that police and other groups should have the power to censor books and movies, 63 per cent felt that Communists should not be allowed to speak on the radio, and 25 per cent agreed that "The government should prohibit some people from making public speeches." [2]

It is an understatement, then, to assert that freedom of speech is itself today a controversial question. It is probably more hotly debated now than when the Founding Fathers voted to adopt the Bill of Rights. There is even considerable dispute within the libertarian camp over how literally or universally the writers of the First Amendment meant their prohibition on the abridgment of free speech to be applied.[3] Though this particular discussion is of great interest

---

[1] John P. Roche, "The Curbing of the Militant Majority," *The Reporter* (July 18, 1963), pp. 35-38.

[2] H. H. Remmers, ed., *Anti-Democratic Attitudes in American Schools*, Northwestern University Press, 1963, pp. 64-66. These findings generally corroborate those of a 1954 national survey of adult opinion conducted by the Gallup Poll and the National Opinion Research Center which found that 68 per cent of the population felt that Communists should not be allowed to speak in their community, 60 per cent that atheists should be prohibited, and 31 per cent that advocates of government ownership of the railroads and big industries should be barred. See Samuel A. Stouffer, *Communism, Conformity and Civil Liberties*, Doubleday & Company, Inc., 1955.

[3] Cf. Leonard Levy, *Legacy of Suppression*, Harvard University Press, 1960 and Hugo Black, "The Bill of Rights," 35 *New York University Law Review* 865 (1960) or in Edmond Cahn, ed., *The Great Rights*, Macmillan, 1963, pp. 43-63.

to scholars, and of considerable importance in discovering precedents for current argument, the crucial question remains, of course, how we shall view the matter today. We cannot and would not want to escape from our history, but it is generally agreed that the marvel of our Constitution is that each generation may breathe new meaning, appropriate to the age, into its abstract principles. In attempting to arrive at decisions on the free speech problems we confront, we can certainly look to the rich experience of our history. We can study the dramatic conflicts of the past—of Socrates, of Galileo, of John Wilkes, and of Peter Zenger. We can read John Milton's *Areopagitica*, the speeches and writings of Jefferson and Madison, and Mill's "On Liberty." But ultimately we must face and resolve the issues in their contemporary context. As Zechariah Chafee, Jr., America's leading twentieth-century authority on free speech, pointed out before his death, most of the law we need to know has been made since 1917.[4] It is with these cases that we shall be principally concerned in this volume.

Our scope will be limited to the United States, not out of any lack of interest in the practices and problems of other societies, but because this is all that can be managed in one short book. Our focus will be on the freedom or control of speech, defined primarily as the communication of ideas and feelings via public speaking, the theater, motion pictures, radio, and television. But because of their inseparable relationship to speech, we shall be concerned, too, with certain aspects of the press, and with handbills, picket signs, and silent demonstrations.

The boundaries thus drawn are still too wide for comprehensive coverage to be possible in the pages that follow. It has been necessary further to exclude certain specialized areas of the subject. Alleged slander and libel, except when directed at public officials rather than private citizens, have been set outside our province. So too, except for a few cases involving general principles, have the rather particularized issues related to labor-management disputes (picketing, boycotts, union and antiunion solicitations), contempt of

---

[4] Zechariah Chafee, Jr., *Free Speech in the United States,* Harvard University Press, 1948, p. 437.

court controversies, and problems arising in the course of Congressional committee investigations of alleged subversive activities.

Attention has been concentrated, instead, on three broad areas which include most of the major cases of the twentieth century—speech that inflames an audience and creates a danger of disorder; speech that is viewed as a threat to national survival; and speech that is regarded as corrupting to public morality. Although there are close relationships among these areas, they are dealt with at first in three separate chapters and brought together again in a fourth.

Coursing throughout the entire discussion will be found a distinction between two broad categories of problems. Free speech controversies of any kind may arise and be dealt with at two significantly different points in time: prior to the act of communication and after the fact. To suppress ideas before they are communicated is known as previous or prior restraint and raises quite different questions from punishing a communicator after he has disseminated his message. Both, to be sure, are interferences with unlimited expression and their ultimate effects may be identical. Hence, the story related by Galsworthy:

> The other day in Russia an Englishman came on a street-meeting shortly after the first revolution had begun. An extremist was addressing the gathering and telling them that they were fools to go on fighting, that they ought to refuse and go home, and so forth. The crowd grew angry, and some soldiers were for making a rush at him; but the chairman, a big burly peasant, stopped them with these words: "Brothers, you know that our country is now a country of free speech. We must listen to this man, we must let him say anything he will. But, brothers, when he's finished, we'll bash his head in." [5]

Our law, like this peasant, makes a distinction between prior restraint and *post facto* punishment, and the implications must constantly be kept in mind when we proceed, as we now do, to an examination of the cases.

[5] John Galsworthy, "American and Briton," 8 *Yale Law Review* 27 (1918).

FREEDOM OF SPEECH

Issues and Cases

Provocation to Anger and the Problem of Preserving the Peace

"It is time enough for the rightful purposes of civil government for its officers to interfere when principles break out into overt acts against peace and good order."

—Thomas Jefferson,
Virginia Statute
Establishing Religious Freedom

TWO ILLINOIS STORIES

Cairo is a small city at the southern tip of Illinois. It lies farther south than St. Louis, Missouri, or Richmond, Virginia. In the summer and fall of 1962 the demonstrations against racial segregation that were spreading across the country reached into Cairo as well. The city fathers responded, on September 10, 1962, by enacting an ordinance making "parades" upon "the public streets" without a permit illegal. Parades were defined as "any organized movement or public procession of people . . . with or without banners or signs . . . for public display or show." Public streets were defined to include not only roadways, but also "sidewalks and the areas between the sidewalks and the curbs." Shortly after the passage of this ordinance some thirty young people were arrested and jailed for its violation when they sought to conduct a peaceful civil rights demonstration on the Cairo streets.

Chicago has, for the past two decades, been one of the nation's centers of racist agitation and controversy. At about 6:20 P.M. on March 22, 1962, three young men, members of the White Youth Corps, an affiliate of the American Nazi Party, appeared in front of the State-Lake Theatre in the heart of the downtown area and proceeded peacefully and quietly to picket the movie that was then playing, *Sergeants Three*, featuring Sammy Davis, Jr. Their signs carried such inscriptions as, "How to be a Jew, lesson number 1 by Sammy the Kosher Coon" and "Sammy Davis Jewnior is a race mixer." A crowd of about one hundred people gathered, many mumbling and cursing at the pickets. A police officer finally ordered the pickets to disperse, and, when they refused, arrested them. They were tried and convicted in a local court on a charge of disorderly conduct.

These incidents, both involving the peaceful expression of a minority viewpoint that is unpalatable to the majority of people to whom it is addressed, suggest a number of key issues regarding the permissible scope of freedom of speech:

1. *Does the majority, as represented by elected or appointed public officials, have the right to require individuals to obtain a permit or license in order to use public property to express their views? If so, under what, if any, circumstances can such permits be denied?*
2. *If no permit is required, may other methods, such as interference at the discretion of the police or a court injunction, be employed to prevent individuals, prior to the act, from expressing or disseminating their beliefs?*
3. *Does an individual or a group have the right to disobey a law that later may be regarded by the courts as an unconstitutional abridgment of free speech?*
4. *Is there a certain kind of speech which, because it offends the audience, arouses their anger, or provokes*

them to violence, may be stopped by police, and may cause the speaker to be punished for his behavior?

———————

Questions of this kind were first approached by the U. S. Supreme Court in 1897 in a case involving the use of the Boston Common for speaking purposes (Davis v. Massachusetts, 167 US 43). In passing on the validity of an ordinance requiring permits for such gatherings, the Court, at that time, held that, just as a man has a right to control the use of his private property in any way he wishes, so has the government a right to regulate the use of the parks, streets, sidewalks, and public halls in any way that its legislature sees fit. But that doctrine was substantially modified in 1939, as we shall see in this chapter (Hague v. C.I.O.), and the power of the state to regulate speech on public property can now be understood only in the light of a whole series of court decisions since that time, which we shall examine.

Similarly, beginning with the case of Near v. Minnesota in 1931 and proceeding through a series of related decisions to Times Film v. Chicago thirty years later, it is necessary to explore the entire development of the Supreme Court's thinking to understand fully our present status regarding the practice of prior restraint of expression.

We shall also discover that our courts have not been altogether consistent in their decisions as to what kinds of speech may or may not be punished after the fact. We will find, instead, a sharp cleavage of opinion, with at times one view prevailing and at times another, over whether it is the speaker or the audience who should be restrained in situations where heated words may spill over into a fight.

The first definitive statement by the U. S. Supreme Court on prior censorship as a general principle, and in particular the use of court injunctions to that end, came in Near v. Minnesota, a case that is cited to the present day as a prevailing precedent in this field. A periodical known as The Saturday Press, published in Minneapolis, was charged with carrying "malicious, scandalous and defamatory articles" about the mayor, other public officials, and the "Jewish race." *The county attorney sought and obtained a court injunction against further dissemination of the journal, under a statute which is described in the opinion below.*

NEAR v. MINNESOTA[1]

MR. CHIEF JUSTICE HUGHES delivered the opinion of the Court.

. . . The statute is not aimed at the redress of individual or private wrongs. Remedies for libel remain available and unaffected. . . . It is aimed at the distribution of scandalous matter as "detrimental to public morals and to the general welfare," tending "to disturb the peace of the community". . . . In the present case, we have no occasion to inquire as to the permissible scope of subsequent punishment. . . . As has been noted, the statute in question does not deal with punishments; it provides for no punishment, except in case of contempt for violation of the court's order, but for suppression and injunction, that is, for restraint upon publication.

The objection has . . . been made that the principle as to immunity from previous restraint is stated too broadly, if every such restraint is deemed to be prohibited. That is undoubtedly true; the protection even as to previous restraint is not absolutely unlimited. But the limitation has been recognized only in exceptional cases. . . .

Judgment reversed.

The Court felt that although prior restraint of communication is not absolutely forbidden, it may be exercised only in the most unusual circumstances. The Saturday Press, it was decided, posed no such circumstances.

———◆———

Dirk De Jonge, a Communist, was indicted under the Oregon Syndicalism Act for assisting in the conduct of a 1934 public meeting in Portland to protest the police shooting of some striking longshoremen and police raids on workers' homes and halls. He, and the others who addressed

---

[1] 283 US 697 (1931).

the meeting, spoke only on these subjects. Nevertheless, De
Jonge was convicted and sentenced to seven years in prison.
The U. S. Supreme Court unanimously reversed the Oregon
decision and took the occasion to recognize peaceable assembly as a right entitled to the same protections as freedom of speech. The Court also attempted to reinforce the
distinction, which is often neglected, between guilt by
association and guilt by unlawful behavior.

DE JONGE v. OREGON [2]

MR. CHIEF JUSTICE HUGHES delivered the opinion of the
Court.

. . . The right of peaceable assembly is a right cognate
to those of free speech and free press and is equally fundamental. . . . peaceable assembly for lawful discussion
cannot be made a crime. The holding of meetings for
peaceable political action cannot be proscribed. Those who
assist in the conduct of such meetings cannot be branded as
criminals on that score. The question, if the rights of free
speech and peaceable assembly are to be preserved, is not as
to the auspices under which the meeting is held but as to
its purpose; not as to the relations of the speakers, but
whether their utterances transcend the bounds of the freedom of speech which the Constitution protects. If the persons assembling have committed crimes elsewhere, if they
have formed or are engaged in a conspiracy against the public peace and order, they may be prosecuted for their conspiracy or other violation of valid laws. But it is a different
matter when the State, instead of prosecuting them for
such offenses, seizes upon mere participation in a peaceable
assembly and a lawful public discussion as the basis for a
criminal charge.

◆

Griffin, Georgia, had an ordinance which forbade the distribution of literature of any kind without first obtaining
written permission from the City Manager. Alma Lovell, a
Jehovah's Witness, proceeded to distribute her religious

---

[2] 299 US 353 (1937).

tracts without the required license and was arrested and sent to jail for fifty days in default of payment of a $50 fine.

The U. S. Supreme Court in 1938, unmoved by Griffin's arguments that it needed a way of keeping its streets free from litter, and that there was no evidence a permit would have been denied if sought, unanimously found the ordinance unconstitutional and reversed the conviction. Although suggesting that such an ordinance might be valid if it left less discretion to public officials and simply attempted some control as to time and place of communications, the Court's condemnation of Griffin's broad restraint was unequivocal. The decision apparently took for granted that Alma Lovell could permissibly violate this unconstitutional law—a position that we shall find repeated and also seemingly qualified in later cases.

LOVELL v. GRIFFIN [3]

MR. CHIEF JUSTICE HUGHES delivered the opinion of the Court.

. . . The ordinance prohibits the distribution of literature of any kind at any time, at any place, and in any manner without a permit from the City Manager.

We think that the ordinance is invalid on its face. Whatever the motive which induced its adoption, its character is such that it strikes at the very foundation of the freedom of the press by subjecting it to license and censorship. . . .

The liberty of the press is not confined to newspapers and periodicals. It necessarily embraces pamphlets and leaflets. These indeed have been historic weapons in the defense of liberty, as the pamphlets of Thomas Paine and others in our own history abundantly attest.

The power of a government to restrain communicators by the requirement of a permit was again brought into question when the Committee for Industrial Organization challenged Mayor Frank "I Am the Law" Hague's iron control

[3] 303 US 444 (1938).

of public speaking in Jersey City, New Jersey. The union, having been repeatedly frustrated in its attempts to obtain permits for its labor organizers to promote their cause in the city, sought and won an injunction from the federal district court against enforcement of the licensing ordinance. The U. S. Supreme Court, in a 5-2 decision in 1939, rejected the city's appeal, and in so doing seemed also to reject the position it had taken many years before in the Boston Common case, that a city government has virtually unlimited authority over the use of public places.

HAGUE v. COMMITTEE FOR INDUSTRIAL ORGANIZATION [4]

MR. JUSTICE ROBERTS:

. . . We have no occasion to determine whether, on the facts disclosed, the *Davis Case* was rightly decided, but we cannot agree that it rules the instant case. Wherever the title of streets and parks may rest, they have immemorially been held in trust for the use of the public and, time out of mind, have been used for purposes of assembly, communicating thoughts between citizens, and discussing public questions. Such use of the streets and public places has, from ancient times, been a part of the privileges, immunities, rights, and liberties of citizens. The privilege of a citizen of the United States to use the streets and parks for communication of views on national questions may be regulated in the interest of all; it is not absolute, but relative, and must be exercised in subordination to the general comfort and convenience, and in consonance with peace and good order; but it must not, in the guise of regulation, be abridged or denied.

We think the court below was right in holding the ordinance void on its face. It does not make comfort or convenience in the use of streets or parks the standard of official action. It enables the Director of Safety to refuse a permit on his mere opinion that such refusal will prevent "riots, disturbances or disorderly assemblage." It can thus, as the record discloses, be made the instrument of arbitrary sup-

---

[4] 307 US 496 (1939).

pression of free expression of views on national affairs for the prohibition of all speaking will undoubtedly "prevent" such eventualities. But uncontrolled official suppression of the privilege cannot be made a substitute for the duty to maintain order in connection with the exercise of the right. . . .

A document that may have had significant influence on the outcome of Hague v. C.I.O. was a "friend of the court" brief submitted by the Bill of Rights Committee of the American Bar Association.

Bill of Rights Committee:[5]

We desire to stress the importance of open-air meetings as a means for public discussion and education. Outdoor public assemblies have a special function in the field of free expression that is fulfilled by no other medium. . . . indispensable in giving free public debate its traditional scope. . . .

The outdoor meeting is especially well adapted to the promotion of unpopular causes, since such causes are likely to command little financial support and therefore must often be promoted by persons who do not have the financial means to "hire a hall" or purchase time on the radio.

Moreover, the outdoor public meeting forms part of the tradition of American life. The Lincoln-Douglas debates were held in the open, and notwithstanding the development of the radio, it still remains true that a large part of our political, economic and social discussion goes on in outdoor meetings. Such meetings in public places are free not only to the speakers but to their audiences. Especially in summer, it is easier in many communities to attract an audience at an open-air meeting than in any other way. . . .

The informal character of the outdoor meeting is often of advantage in developing questions and answers. . . . it

---

[5] Excerpts from the *amicus curiae* brief submitted to the U. S. Supreme Court in *Hague* v. *C.I.O.,* 307 US 496, by the Bill of Rights Committee of the American Bar Association.

may fairly be said that the outdoor meeting is the most *democratic* forum of expression.

It is important to recognize that *as a practical matter* a city has a virtual monopoly of every open space at which a considerable outdoor meeting can be held. . . . If, therefore, a city can constitutionally close *both* its streets and its parks entirely to public meetings, the practical result would make impossible any open-air meetings in any large city. . . . Such a result would, it seems plain, amount to an unconstitutional abridgement of the rights of free speech and assembly. It follows, we contend, that a city *must* make some reasonable provision for the holding of outdoor public meetings.

. . . A city may regulate reasonably in this respect but may not arbitrarily discriminate. This does not mean that the city is unable to make any choices. Thus it can keep adults out of children's playgrounds. But it cannot keep out red-headed children while admitting youthful blondes and brunettes, nor can it limit the park benches to members of one political party. . . . there is, we submit, a constitutional difference between reasonable regulation and arbitrary exclusion. . . .

The danger of the private ownership theory of public property, represented by *Davis* v. *Massachusetts*, becomes particularly impressive at a time like the present when acquisitions of large amounts of property are being made by government. . . .

The true analogy to government ownership of parks and other property dedicated to public uses is furnished by a public utility, which must give service to all so long as this is consistent with the performance of its functions. It can regulate, but not discriminate.

. . . some danger of disorder must be faced for the sake of the constitutional right of free assembly. It is natural that threats of trouble should often accompany meetings on controversial questions. But it is not consistent with American principles to suppress the meetings on that account. The practice under ordinary conditions in our large cities is for the authorities to arrange with the applicants to

put the meeting in a suitable place, and have enough policemen on hand to quell apprehended disturbances. . . .
Otherwise these rights of the people to meet and of speakers to address the citizens so gathered, could not merely be
"abridged" but could be destroyed by the action of a small
minority of persons hostile to the speakers or to the views
they would be likely to express. . . . It is the duty of the
officials to prevent or suppress the threatened disorder with
a firm hand instead of timidly yielding to threats.

"The right of the people peaceably to assemble" cannot
mean that the right ceases unless everybody present, including opponents of the speakers, is certain to be peaceable.
Law-abiding speakers and their supporters should not be
deprived of the great American institution of assemblage in
the open air because other persons are intolerant and ready
to violate the law against assault and battery. Such a doctrine would mean that a citizen loses his constitutional
rights because his opponent threatens to commit crimes.

Surely a speaker ought not to be suppressed because his
opponents propose to use violence. It is they who should
suffer for their lawlessness, not he. Let the threateners be
arrested for assault, or at least put under bonds to keep the
peace.

*To those who may have been concerned about the prac-
ticality, from a law enforcement officer's point of view, of
the bar association and Supreme Court position in Hague v.
C.I.O., Professor Zechariah Chafee proposed an interesting
possible solution.*

Zechariah Chafee, Jr.:[6]

The result of the Hague decision seems to be that speakers are free to talk without previous permission from anybody, but remain fully responsible for what they say. If it
be thought there is danger that without a permit the police

[6] Reprinted by permission of the publishers from Zechariah Chafee,
Jr., *Free Speech in the United States* (Cambridge, Mass.: Harvard University Press), pp. 430-31. Copyright, 1941, by the President and Fellows of Harvard College.

would not know of the speech so as to be on hand in case of trouble it would be practicable to adopt a plan which worked well in Republican France. The prospective speaker does not apply for a permit, he merely notifies the city authorities that he is going to speak. They then send him a receipt, which they can be legally compelled by him to do if they will not send it voluntarily. This receipt can be shown to any policeman as evidence that the meeting is legal. His notice serves as a warning to the city to have as many policemen on hand as seem desirable under the circumstances, and allows them to assign a suitable place for the meeting.

The problems of prior restraint and post facto punishment merged into a single case when Newton Cantwell and his sons, Jesse and Russell, members of Jehovah's Witnesses, were arrested in New Haven, Connecticut. The Cantwells had gone to Cassius Street, where some 90 per cent of the residents were Roman Catholic, and had approached individuals asking their permission to play a phonograph record to them. If permission was granted they would proceed with the record, which consisted of an attack on the Catholic religion.

The Cantwells were convicted on two counts, both reversed by the U. S. Supreme Court in 1940. The first was for violation of a state statute which forbade solicitation for any religious cause without government certification. The second was for the common law offense of inciting a breach of the peace.

CANTWELL v. CONNECTICUT [7]

MR. JUSTICE ROBERTS delivered the opinion of the Court. . . . First. We hold that the statute, as construed and applied to the appellants, deprives them of their liberty without due process of law in contravention of the Fourteenth Amendment. . . . No one would contest the proposition that a State may not, by statute, wholly deny the

---

[7] 310 US 296 (1940).

right to preach or to disseminate religious views. . . . It is equally clear that a State may by general and non-discriminatory legislation regulate the times, places, and the manner of soliciting upon its streets, and of holding meetings thereon. . . . The appellants are right in their insistence that the Act in question is not such a regulation. . . . amounts to a prior restraint on the exercise of their religion within the meaning of the Constitution. . . .

The general regulation, in the public interest, of solicitation, which does not involve any religious test . . . is not open to any constitutional objection. . . .

It will be noted, however, that the Act requires an application to the secretary of the public welfare council of the State; that he is empowered to determine whether the cause is a religious one. . . . If he finds that the cause is not that of religion, to solicit for it becomes a crime. . . .

The State asserts that if the licensing officer acts arbitrarily, capriciously, or corruptly, his action is subject to judicial correction. . . .

To this suggestion there are several sufficient answers. The line between a discretionary and a ministerial act is not always easy to mark and the statute has not been construed by the state court to impose a mere ministerial duty on the secretary of the welfare council. Upon his decision as to the nature of the cause, the right to solicit depends. Moreover, the availability of a judicial remedy for abuses in the system of licensing still leaves that system one of previous restraint which, in the field of free speech and press, we have held inadmissible. . . .

Second. We hold that, in the circumstances disclosed, the conviction of Jesse Cantwell on the fifth count must be set aside. . . .

The offense known as breach of the peace embraces a great variety of conduct destroying or menacing public order and tranquility. . . . No one would have the hardihood to suggest that the principle of freedom of speech sanctions incitement to riot or that religious liberty connotes the privilege to exhort others to physical attack upon those belonging to another sect. When clear and present danger of riot, disorder, interference with traffic upon the public streets, or other immediate threat to public safety, peace, or order, appears, the power of the State to prevent or punish is obvious. Equally obvious is that a State may not unduly suppress free communication of views, religious or other, under the guise of conserving desirable conditions. . . .

Cantwell's conduct, in the view of the court below, considered apart from the effect of his communication upon his hearers, did not amount to a breach of the peace. One may, however, be guilty of the offense if he commits acts or makes statements likely to provoke violence and disturbance of good order, even though no such eventuality be intended. Decisions to this effect are many, but examination discloses that, in practically all, the provocative language which was held to amount to a breach of the peace consisted of profane, indecent, or abusive remarks directed to the person of the hearer. Resort to epithets or personal abuse is not in any proper sense communication of information or opinion safeguarded by the Constitution, and its punishment as a criminal act would raise no question under that instrument.

We find in the instant case no assault or threatening of bodily harm, no truculent bearing, no intentional discourtesy, no personal abuse. . . .

In the realm of religious faith, and in that of political belief, sharp differences arise. In both fields, the tenets of one man may seem the rankest error to his neighbor. To persuade others to his own point of view, the pleader, as we know, at times, resorts to exaggeration, to vilification of men who have been, or are, prominent in church or state, and even to false statement. But the people of this nation have ordained in the light of history, that, in spite of the probability of excesses and abuses, these liberties are, in the long view, essential to enlightened opinion and right conduct on the part of the citizens of a democracy.

The essential characteristic of these liberties is, that under their shield many types of life, character, opinion and belief can develop unmolested and unobstructed. Nowhere is this shield more necessary than in our own country for a people composed of many races and of many creeds.

There are limits to the exercise of these liberties. The danger in these times from the coercive activities of those who in the delusion of racial or religious conceit would incite violence and breaches of the peace in order to deprive others of their equal right to the exercise of their liberties, is emphasized by events familiar to all. These and other transgressions of those limits the States appropriately may punish.

The position taken here by the Court on the question of prior restraint followed quite logically from Lovell and Hague. Reasonable regulations as to time, place and prior notification are permissible, but rules which make possible arbitrary or prejudicial government restraints on speech are not.

Unfortunately, the Court's position on the breach of peace issue was not nearly so clear. The opinion affirmed on the one hand that, in religious and political discussion, one may permissibly resort to "exaggeration" and "vilification" and not be punished because listeners are made angry. But it then turned around and suggested that "epithets" and "personal abuse" are out of bounds, and that arousing anger in an audience might indeed be so provocative of violence as to be punishable.

How this blurred line might be drawn in future cases was revealed two years later when another Jehovah's Witness spoke unkind words to a police officer.

CHAPLINSKY v. NEW HAMPSHIRE [8]

Mr. Justice Murphy delivered the opinion of the Court.

Appellant, a member of the sect known as Jehovah's Witnesses, was convicted in the municipal court of Rochester, New Hampshire, for violation of . . . the Public Laws of New Hampshire:

No person shall address any offensive, derisive or annoying word to any other person who is lawfully in

[8] 315 US 568 (1942).

any street or other public place, nor call him by any offensive or derisive name. . . .

The complaint charged that appellant . . . did unlawfully repeat, the words following, addressed to the complainant, that is to say, "You are a God damned racketeer" and "a damned Fascist and the whole government of Rochester are Fascists or agents of Fascists." . . .

There was no substantial dispute over the facts. Chaplinsky was distributing the literature of his sect on the streets. . . . Members of the local citizenry complained to the City Marshal, Bowering. . . . Bowering told them that Chaplinsky was lawfully engaged and then warned Chaplinsky that the crowd was getting restless. Some time later . . . Bowering repeated his earlier warning to Chaplinsky who then addressed to Bowering the words set forth in the complaint. . . .

Allowing the broadest scope to the language and purpose of the Fourteenth Amendment, it is well understood that the right of free speech is not absolute at all times and under all circumstances. There are certain well-defined and narrowly limited classes of speech, the prevention and punishment of which have never been thought to raise any constitutional problem. These include the lewd and obscene, the profane, the libelous, and the insulting or "fighting" words—those which by their very utterance inflict injury or tend to incite an immediate breach of the peace. It has been well observed that such utterances are no essential part of any exposition of ideas, and are of such slight social value as a step to truth that any benefit that may be derived from them is clearly outweighed by the social interest in order and morality. . . . the state court declared . . .

The word "offensive" is not to be defined in terms of what a particular addressee thinks. . . . The test is what men of common intelligence would understand would be words likely to cause an average addressee to fight. . . . The English language has a number of words and expressions which by general consent are "fighting words" when said without a disarming

smile. . . . Such words, as ordinary men know, are
likely to cause a fight. So are threatening, profane or
obscene revilings. . . .

We are unable to say that the limited scope of the statute as thus construed contravenes the Constitutional right
of free expression. . . .
Affirmed.

*It is rather surprising, in view of the large chunks carved
out of the First Amendment by this decision, that the
opinion was rendered on behalf of a unanimous court. Not
only are obscene, profane and libelous words declared un-
acceptable, but the social value of an utterance (as determined, presumably, by the courts) is suggested as a test of
its permissibility, as are the emotional reactions of an audience. As we shall see in later cases, this "fighting words"
doctrine of the Chaplinsky decision probably departed farther from a libertarian position than some of the Court
intended to go, for it is invoked again only when conven-
ient, and conveniently set aside when a court majority finds
it in the way.*

---

*The license requirement issue arose in new form when
the president of the United Automobile Workers, C.I.O.,
sought to address a labor meeting in Houston without first
obtaining the union organizer's card required for such purposes by Texas law. Upon learning of Thomas' declared intention to speak without registering as required, the state
attorney general obtained a court order, which was served
upon Thomas, restraining him from acting in this way. He
delivered his speech nonetheless, and was convicted for
contempt of court. The conviction was upheld by the Supreme Court of Texas, but reversed in 1945 by a 5-4 vote
of the U. S. Supreme Court. The majority, proclaiming
that the First Amendment holds a preferred place in our
scheme of government, declared that requiring previous
registration to make a lawful public speech was unconstitutional as applied in this case, and that Thomas' punish-*

ment for violating the court's restraining order could not stand. The minority argued that since the law in question "is a registration statute and nothing more," and "confers only 'ministerial and not discretionary powers' upon the Secretary of State," the government had not exceeded its constitutional authority in the case.

THOMAS v. COLLINS [9]

MR. JUSTICE RUTLEDGE delivered the opinion of the Court.

. . . The case confronts us again with the duty our system places on this Court to say where the individual's freedom ends and the State's power begins. Choice on that border, now as always delicate, is perhaps more so where the usual presumption supporting legislation is balanced by the preferred place given in our scheme to the great, the indispensable democratic freedoms secured by the First Amendment. . . . any attempt to restrict those liberties must be justified by clear public interest, threatened not doubtfully or remotely, but by clear and present danger. . . . Only the gravest abuses, endangering paramount interests, give occasion for permissible limitation. It is therefore in our tradition to allow the widest room for discussion, the narrowest range for its restriction, particularly when this right is exercised in conjunction with peaceable assembly. It was not by accident or coincidence that the rights to freedom in speech and press were coupled in a single guaranty with the rights of the people peaceably to assemble and to petition for redress of grievances. All these, though not identical, are inseparable.

The problem of regulating speech in the interests of community order or individual privacy continued to plague the Court in two difficult cases involving the use of loud-speakers mounted on sound trucks. The first instance, in 1948, centered on an ordinance of Lockport, New York, which forbade the use of loud-speakers except by permission

[9] 323 US 516 (1945).

of the Chief of Police. Saia, a minister of Jehovah's Witnesses, had obtained such a permit and made use of it on a number of Sundays in a public park. When the permit expired, however, he was denied another one because complaints had been made. He went ahead in spite of this and used his amplification equipment on four additional occasions, whereupon he was convicted for violation of the ordinance. The U. S. Supreme Court, in a 5-4 split, struck down the ordinance as granting too much discretion to the police.

But the following year, in a case coming from Trenton, New Jersey, the Court took a seemingly different stance. This time the city ordinance did not require a license; it simply barred from use on public streets any sound amplifiers emitting "loud and raucous noises." In another 5-4 decision the Supreme Court this time sustained the ordinance and a conviction based upon it. But the ordinance and its implications were interpreted so variously by the justices that they could not agree on the phrasing of a single Court opinion. It was clear that most felt a municipality could not entirely bar all loud-speakers from the community, but that reasonable regulation would be justified. What constituted reasonable regulation, however, was left quite muddy. For example, might loud-speakers be barred entirely from the streets if permitted in parks? How loud could an amplifier be without being "loud and raucous"? And was Trenton's law an absolute prohibition or a reasonable regulation? The average layman can be forgiven if, after reading the opinions below, he is still not quite sure of the answers to these questions.

SAIA v. NEW YORK [10]

Opinion of the Court by MR. JUSTICE DOUGLAS announced by MR. JUSTICE BLACK.

. . . Loud-speakers are today indispensable instruments of effective public speech. The sound truck has become an accepted method of political campaigning. It is the way people are reached. Must a candidate for governor or the

---

[10] 334 US 558 (1948).

Congress depend on the whim or caprice of the Chief of
Police in order to use his sound truck for campaigning?
Must he prove to the satisfaction of that official that his
noise will not be annoying to people? . . .

Any abuses which loud-speakers create can be controlled
by narrowly drawn statutes. When a city allows an official
to ban them in his uncontrolled discretion it sanctions a
device for suppression of free communication of ideas. In
this case a permit is denied because some persons were said
to have found the sound annoying. In the next one a permit may be denied because some people find the ideas annoying. Annoyance at ideas can be cloaked in annoyance at
sound.

MR. JUSTICE FRANKFURTER, with whom MR. JUSTICE
REED and MR. JUSTICE BURTON concur, dissenting.

. . . The native power of human speech can interfere
little with the self-protection of those who do not wish to
listen. They may easily move beyond earshot, just as those
who do not choose to read need not have their attention
bludgeoned by undesired reading matter. . . . But modern devices for amplifying the range and volume of the
voice, or its recording, afford easy, too easy, opportunities
for aural aggression. If uncontrolled, the result is intrusion
into cherished privacy. . . . Surely there is not a constitutional right to force unwilling people to listen. . . . It is
not unconstitutional for a State to vest in a public official
the determination of what is in effect a nuisance merely
because such authority may be outrageously misused by trying to stifle the expression of some undesired opinion under
the meretricious cloak of a nuisance. Judicial remedies are
available for such abuse of authority.

KOVACS v. COOPER [11]

MR. JUSTICE REED announced the judgment of the Court
and an opinion in which the CHIEF JUSTICE and MR. JUS-
TICE BURTON join.

. . . Unrestrained use throughout a municipality of all
sound amplifying devices would be intolerable. . . . We

---

[11] 336 US 77 (1949).

accept the determination of New Jersey that §4 applies only to vehicles with sound amplifiers emitting loud and raucous noises. . . . We think it is a permissible exercise of legislative discretion to bar sound trucks with broadcasts of public interest, amplified to a loud and raucous volume, from the public ways of municipalities.

MR. JUSTICE BLACK, with whom MR. JUSTICE DOUGLAS, and MR. JUSTICE RUTLEDGE concur, dissenting.

. . . The New Jersey ordinance is on its face, and as construed and applied in this case by that state's courts, an absolute and unqualified prohibition of amplifying devices on any of Trenton's streets at any time, at any place, for any purpose, and without regard to how noisy they may be. . . .

There are many people who have ideas that they wish to disseminate but who do not have enough money to own or control publishing plants, newspapers, radios, moving picture studios, or chains of show places. Yet everybody knows the vast reaches of these powerful channels of communication which from the very nature of our economic system must be under the control and guidance of comparatively few people. On the other hand, public speaking is done by many men of divergent minds with no centralized control over the ideas they entertain so as to limit the causes they espouse. It is no reflection on the value of preserving freedom for dissemination of the ideas of publishers of newspapers, magazines, and other literature, to believe that transmission of ideas through public speaking is also essential to the sound thinking of a fully informed citizenry.

It is of particular importance in a government where people elect their officials that the fullest opportunity be afforded candidates to express and voters to hear their views. It is of equal importance that criticism of governmental action not be limited to criticisms by press, radio, and moving pictures. In no other way except public speaking can the desirable objective of widespread public discussion be assured. For the press, the radio, and the moving picture owners have their favorites, and it assumes the impossible to suppose that these agencies will at all times be equally fair as between the candidates and officials they favor and those whom they vigorously oppose. And it is an obvious fact that public speaking today without the sound amplifiers is a wholly inadequate way to reach the people on a large scale. Consequently, to tip the scales against transmission of ideas through public speaking, as the Court does today, is to deprive the people of a large part of the basic advantages of the receipt of ideas that the First Amendment was designed to protect.

There is no more reason that I can see for wholly prohibiting one useful instrument of communication than another. If Trenton can completely bar the streets to the advantageous use of loud-speakers, all cities can do the same. In that event preference in the dissemination of ideas is given those who can obtain the support of newspapers, etc., or those who have money enough to buy advertising from newspapers, radios, or moving pictures. This Court should no more permit this invidious prohibition against the dissemination of ideas by speaking than it would permit a complete blackout of the press, the radio, or moving pictures. It is wise for all who cherish freedom of expression to reflect upon the plain fact that a holding that the audiences of public speakers can be constitutionally prohibited is not unrelated to a like prohibition in other fields. And the right to freedom of expression should be protected from absolute censorship for persons without, as for persons with, wealth and power. At least, such is the theory of our society.

I am aware that the "blare" of this new method of carrying ideas is susceptible of abuse and may under certain circumstances constitute an intolerable nuisance. But ordinances can be drawn which adequately protect a community from unreasonable use of public speaking devices without absolutely denying to the community's citizens all information that may be disseminated or received through this new avenue for trade in ideas. I would agree without reservation to the sentiment that "unrestrained use throughout a municipality of all sound amplifying devices would be intolerable." And of course cities may restrict or absolutely ban the use of amplifiers on busy streets in the business area. A city ordinance that reasonably restricts the volume of sound, or the hours during which an amplifier may be used, does not, in my mind, infringe the constitutionally protected area of free speech. It is because this ordinance does none of these things, but is instead an absolute prohibition of all uses of an amplifier on any of the streets of Trenton at any time that I must dissent.

I would reverse the judgment.

———————◆———————

There is at least one free speech issue on which the U. S. Supreme Court has always been clear and consistent. When speech is part and parcel of otherwise illegal action it is not entitled to protection by the First Amendment just because it happens to be speech. This principle has been recognized in numerous cases before the Court, and on one occasion, in a labor picketing dispute, was enunciated by the most libertarian member of that bench.

GIBONEY v. EMPIRE STORAGE AND ICE COMPANY [12]

MR. JUSTICE BLACK delivered the opinion of the Court.

. . . It is contended that the injunction against picketing adjacent to Empire's place of business is an unconstitutional abridgment of free speech because the picketers were attempting peacefully to publicize truthful facts about a labor dispute. . . .

It rarely has been suggested that the constitutional freedom of speech and press extends its immunity to speech or writing used as an integral part of conduct in violation of a valid criminal statute. We reject the contention now. . . .

We think the circumstances here and the reasons advanced by the Missouri courts justify restraint of the picketing which was done in violation of Missouri's valid law. . . . the placards were to effectuate the purposes of an unlawful combination, and their sole, unlawful immediate objective was to induce Empire to violate the Missouri law. . . . it has never been deemed an abridgment of freedom of speech or press to make a course of conduct illegal merely because the conduct was in part initiated, evidenced, or carried out by means of language, either spoken,

---

[12] 336 US 490 (1949).

written, or printed. Such an expansive interpretation of the constitutional guaranties of speech and press would make it practically impossible ever to enforce laws against agreements in restraint of trade as well as many other agreements and conspiracies deemed injurious to society. . . .

———————◆———————

One of the most dramatic free speech events with which the courts have ever had to deal occurred one turbulent evening in an auditorium in Chicago. Father Terminiello, a Catholic priest under suspension by his bishop, had come from Birmingham, Alabama, to spew forth his message of racial and religious hatred to some eight hundred sympathizers in the hall. Over one thousand demonstrators had gathered outside to protest and ultimately to hurl bricks, bottles, and stink bombs. There was no problem here of prior restraint for, despite the tumultuous situation, a cordon of police maintained sufficient control of the situation that Terminiello was able to deliver his entire speech. But he was arrested thereafter and convicted of inciting a breach of the peace.

The question was seemingly a simple one. How far can one go in inflaming a crowd without subjecting himself to punishment by the law? The five-man majority of the U. S. Supreme Court met this issue somewhat tangentially, by taking exception to the broad way in which the trial judge had instructed the jury in what constituted a breach of the peace, and on this basis overruled the Illinois conviction of Terminiello. But Justice Jackson's passionate dissent has perhaps had as much influence on later decisions in this field as the majority opinion.

TERMINIELLO v. CITY OF CHICAGO [13]

MR. JUSTICE DOUGLAS delivered the opinion of the Court.

. . . the statutory words "breach of the peace" were defined in instructions to the jury to include speech which "stirs the public to anger, invites dispute, brings about a

---

[13] 337 US 1 (1949).

condition of unrest, or creates a disturbance. . . ." That construction of the ordinance is a ruling on a question of state law that is as binding on us as though the precise words had been written into the ordinance. . . . a function of free speech under our system of government is to invite dispute. It may indeed best serve its high purpose when it induces a condition of unrest, creates dissatisfaction with conditions as they are, or even stirs people to anger. Speech is often provocative and challenging. It may strike at prejudices and preconceptions and have profound unsettling effects as it presses for acceptance of an idea. That is why freedom of speech, though not absolute, . . . is nevertheless protected against censorship or punishment, unless shown likely to produce a clear and present danger of a serious substantive evil that arises far above public inconvenience, annoyance, or unrest. . . .

MR. JUSTICE JACKSON, dissenting.

The Court reverses this conviction by reiterating generalized approbations of freedom of speech with which, in the abstract, no one will disagree. . . .

But the local court that tried Terminiello was not indulging in theory. It was dealing with a riot and with a speech that provoked a hostile mob and incited a friendly one, and threatened violence between the two. . . . underneath a little issue of Terminiello and his hundred-dollar fine lurk some of the most far-reaching constitutional questions that can confront a people who value both liberty and order. This Court seems to regard these as enemies of each other and to be of the view that we must forego order to achieve liberty. So it fixes its eyes on a conception of freedom of speech so rigid as to tolerate no concession to society's need for public order.

An old proverb warns us to take heed lest we "walk into a well from looking at the stars." . . . The group of which Terminiello is a part claims that his behavior, because it involved a speech, is above the reach of local authorities. If the mild action those authorities have taken is forbidden, it is plain that hereafter there is nothing effective left that they can do. . . . Terminiello's victory today certainly fulfills the most extravagant hopes of both right and left totalitarian groups, who want nothing so much as to paralyze and discredit the only democratic authority that can curb them in their battle for the streets.

I am unable to see that the local authorities have transgressed the Federal Constitution. Illinois imposed no prior censorship or suppression on Terminiello. On the contrary, its sufferance and protection was all that enabled him to speak. . . .

A trial court and jury has found only that in the context of violence and disorder in which it was made, this speech was a provocation to immediate breach of the peace and therefore cannot claim constitutional immunity from punishment. . . .

Rioting is a substantive evil, which I take it no one will deny that the State and the City have the right and the duty to prevent and punish. . . .

Only recently this Court held that a state could punish as a breach of the peace use of epithets such as "damned racketeer" and "damned fascist," addressed to only one person, an official, because likely to provoke the average person to retaliation. But these are mild in comparison to the epithets "slimy scum," "snakes," "bedbugs," and the like, which Terminiello hurled at an already inflamed mob of his adversaries. . . .

Because a subject is legally arguable . . . does not mean that public sentiment will be patient of its advocacy at all times and in all manners. . . . Hence many speeches, such as that of Terminiello, may be legally permissible but may nevertheless in some surroundings, be a menace to peace and order. When conditions show the speaker that this is the case, as it did here, there certainly comes a point beyond which he cannot indulge in provocations to violence without being answerable to society. . . .

But I would not be understood as suggesting that the United States can or should meet this dilemma by suppression of free, open and public speaking on the part of any group or ideology. Suppression has never been a successful permanent policy; any surface serenity that it creates is a false security, while conspirational forces go underground. My confidence in American institutions and in the sound

sense of the American people is such that if with a stroke
of the pen I could silence every fascist and communist
speaker, I would not do it. . . .

This Court has gone far toward accepting the doctrine
that civil liberty means the removal of all restraints from
these crowds and that all local attempts to maintain order
are impairments of the liberty of the citizen. The choice is
not between order and liberty. It is between liberty with
order and anarchy without either. There is danger that, if
the Court does not temper its doctrinaire logic with a little
practical wisdom it will convert the constitutional Bill of
Rights into a suicide pact.

I would affirm the conviction.

*Whether or not one agrees with the Terminiello decision,
it is difficult to reconcile the outcome with the earlier
Chaplinsky case, as was noted by Justice Jackson and is reinforced by the following critical comment.*

Walter Berns:[14]

That his vile denunciations and frenetic harangues were
"fighting words" within the meaning given these by the
Illinois courts and the Supreme Court itself in the Chaplinsky case, and that the situation for which he, along
with his antagonists, was responsible—an estimated fifteen
hundred people in the streets breaking in doors, hurling
bricks, rocks, bottles, and ice picks, tearing at Terminiello's
followers and threatening to hang and kill them; and hun-
dreds more inside listening to Terminiello hurl his epithets
of hate and vilification, and urge them to tolerate no longer
the "slimy scum" outside the hall, while cordons of police
strained to keep the mob outside from beating down the
doors—that this situation was a breach of the peace can
hardly be denied. As Mr. Justice Douglas quaintly put it,
the police "were not able to prevent several disturbances."
. . . While in the Chaplinsky case the Court refused to

---

[14] Reprinted by permission of the publishers from Walter Berns, *Freedom, Virtue and the First Amendment*, pp. 112-14. Copyright © 1957
by the Louisiana State University Press.

concede the contention that the First Amendment protected the "fighting words" of one man hurled at one policeman, here it went out of its way to protect the right of a speaker whose words were "fighting" beyond any spoken by Chaplinsky.

———————

Carl Jacob Kunz was a Baptist minister with a record of ridiculing and denouncing other religious beliefs, particularly those of Catholics and Jews. In conformity with a New York City ordinance that required a police permit to hold public meetings on the streets, Kunz applied for a license, was turned down, and was subsequently arrested for speaking at Columbus Circle. The U. S. Supreme Court in 1951, with only one dissent, followed the pattern established in Near, Lovell, Hague, and Thomas, and declared the ordinance unconstitutional.

KUNZ v. NEW YORK [15]

MR. CHIEF JUSTICE VINSON delivered the opinion of the Court.

. . . We have here, then, an ordinance which gives an administrative official discretionary power to control in advance the right of citizens to speak on religious matters on the streets of New York. As such, the ordinance is clearly invalid as a prior restraint on the exercise of First Amendment rights.

MR. JUSTICE JACKSON, dissenting.

. . . emergencies may arise on streets which would become catastrophes if there was not immediate police action. The crowd which should be tolerant may be prejudiced and angry or malicious. If the situation threatens to get out of hand for the force present, I think the police may require the speaker, even if within his rights, to yield his right temporarily to the greater interest of peace. . . .

Of course, as to the press, there are the best of reasons against any licensing or prior restraint. . . . But precedents from that field cannot reasonably be transposed to the

———————

[15] 340 US 290 (1951).

street-meeting field. The impact of publishing on public order has no similarity with that of a street meeting. Publishing does not make private use of public property. It reaches only those who chose to read, and, in that way, is analogous to a meeting held in a hall where those who come do so by choice. Written words are less apt to incite or provoke to mass action than spoken words, speech being the primitive and direct communication with emotions. Few are the riots caused by publication alone, few are the mobs that have not their immediate origin in harangue.

————◆————

Having apparently turned away from the Chaplinsky "fighting words" doctrine in Terminiello v. Chicago, the Supreme Court moved toward it again two years later. A young college student named Irving Feiner had mounted his soap box on a Syracuse sidewalk and had, among other things, called President Truman a "bum." He also urged his interracial audience of about eighty people, some apparently sympathetic and some hostile, that Negroes "should rise up in arms and fight for their rights." Threats against the speaker were uttered by persons in the crowd, which was growing increasingly restless. A police officer finally asked Feiner to stop talking and when, after three requests, he still refused, the officer arrested him. He was charged and convicted of disorderly conduct. The conviction was sustained by a 6-3 vote.

FEINER v. NEW YORK [16]

Mr. Chief Justice Vinson delivered the opinion of the Court.

. . . We are well aware that the ordinary murmurings and objections of a hostile audience cannot be allowed to silence a speaker, and are also mindful of the possible danger of giving overzealous police officials complete discretion to break up otherwise lawful public meetings. . . . But we are not faced here with such a situation. It is one thing to say that the police cannot be used as an instrument for the

---

[16] 340 US 315 (1951).

suppression of unpopular views, and another to say that, when as here the speaker passes the bounds of argument and persuasion and undertakes incitement to riot, they are powerless to prevent a breach of the peace. . . .

Mr. Justice Black, dissenting.

. . . As to the existence of a dangerous situation on the street corner, it seems farfetched to suggest that the "facts" show any imminent threat of riot or uncontrollable disorder. It is neither unusual nor unexpected that some people at public street meetings mutter, mill about, push, shove, or disagree. . . . Nor does one isolated threat to assault the speaker forebode disorder. . . .

Moreover, assuming that the "facts" did indicate a critical situation, I reject the implication of the Court's opinion that the police had no obligation to protect petitioner's constitutional right to talk. The police of course have power to prevent breaches of the peace. But if, in the name of preserving order, they ever can interfere with a lawful public speaker, they first must make all reasonable efforts to protect him. Here the policeman did not even pretend to try to protect petitioner. . . . Their duty was to protect petitioner's right to talk, even to the extent of arresting the man who threatened to interfere. Instead, they shirked that duty and acted only to suppress the right to speak.

Finally, I cannot agree with the Court's statement that petitioner's disregard of the policeman's unexplained request amounted to such "deliberate defiance" as would justify an arrest or conviction for disorderly conduct. On the contrary, I think that the policeman's action was a "deliberate defiance" of ordinary official duty as well as of the constitutional right of free speech. . . . a man making a lawful address is certainly not required to be silent merely because an officer directs it. Petitioner was entitled to know why he should cease doing a lawful act. Not once was he told. I understand that people in authoritarian countries must obey arbitrary orders. I had hoped that there was no such duty in the United States.

The Kunz and Feiner decisions were handed down by the U. S. Supreme Court on the same day in 1951 as a third

opinion, Niemotko v. Maryland, 340 US 268. This was
another case involving a broadly drawn ordinance requiring
permits to use a public park for meetings, which was unanimously struck down by the Court. Justice Frankfurter wrote
a concurring opinion which combined his comments on all
three cases and which is a landmark of legal scholarship on
freedom of speech. We do not include it here because of its
length and technicality, but simply take note of it as an
excellent source for a summary of the issues and cases in
freedom of speech dealt with to that date.

As antagonisms in the race relations field have grown, attempts by government to ameliorate the conflict have been
increased. One such effort by the Illinois legislature was
what came to be known as a "group libel" law, making it
illegal to speak or write words which exposed "the citizens
of any race, color, creed, or religion to contempt, derision
or obloquy. . . ." The statute received its first Supreme
Court test when Joseph Beauharnais was convicted of its
violation in Chicago for publishing and distributing leaflets
on the downtown streets calling on his fellow Chicagoans
"to prevent the white race from becoming mongrelized by
the negro." This extension of the concept of libel to include
remarks about groups as well as individuals disturbed the
most libertarian members of the Court and, as applied in
this case, Justice Jackson as well. But a majority of five
found nothing unconstitutional about it, although reserving
judgment on its wisdom. The Court also used the occasion
to set forth the far-reaching doctrine that in cases of libel,
obscenity, and other classes of speech that it regarded as
falling outside the protection of the First Amendment, it
is unnecessary to prove the existence of a "clear and present danger" of unlawful results in order to obtain a conviction.

BEAUHARNAIS v. ILLINOIS [17]

MR. JUSTICE FRANKFURTER delivered the opinion of the
Court.

----

[17] 343 US 250 (1952).

. . . if an utterance directed at an individual may be the object of criminal sanctions, we cannot deny to a State power to punish the same utterance directed at a defined group, unless we can say that this is a willful and purposeless restriction unrelated to the peace and well-being of the State. . . .

Libelous utterances, not being within the area of constitutionally protected speech, it is unnecessary, either for us or for the State courts, to consider the issues behind the phrase "clear and present danger." Certainly no one would contend that obscene speech, for example, may be punished only upon a showing of such circumstances. Libel, as we have seen, is in the same class.

. . . our finding that the law is not constitutionally objectionable carries no implication of approval of the wisdom of the legislation or of its efficacy. These questions may raise doubt in our minds as well as in others. It is not for us, however, to make the legislative judgment. We are not at liberty to erect those doubts into fundamental law.

Affirmed.

MR. JUSTICE BLACK, with whom MR. JUSTICE DOUGLAS concurs, dissenting.

. . . the Court . . . acts on the bland assumption that the First Amendment is wholly irrelevant. . . . This follows logically, I suppose, from recent constitutional doctrine which appears to measure state laws solely by this Court's notions of civilized "canons of decency," reasonableness, etc. . . . Under this "reasonableness" test, state laws abridging First Amendment freedoms are sustained if found to have a "rational basis." . . . Today's case degrades First Amendment freedoms to the "rational basis" level. . . .

The Court's holding here and the constitutional doctrine behind it leave the right of assembly, petition, speech and press almost completely at the mercy of state legislative, executive, and judicial agencies. I say "almost" because state curtailment of these freedoms may still be invalidated if a majority of this Court conclude that a particular infringement is "without reason," or is "a willful and purposeless restriction unrelated to the peace and well-being of the State." . . .

Unless I misread history the majority is giving libel a more expansive scope and more respectable status than it was ever accorded even in the Star Chamber. . . . in arguing for or against the enactment of laws that may differently affect huge groups, it is now very dangerous indeed to say something critical of one of the groups. . . .

No rationalization on a purely legal level can conceal the fact that state laws like this one present a constant overhanging threat to freedom of speech, press and religion. . . . the same kind of state law that makes Beauharnais a criminal for advocating segregation in Illinois can be utilized to send people to jail in other states for advocating equality and nonsegregation. What Beauharnais said in his leaflet is mild compared with usual arguments on both sides of racial controversies. . . .

If there be minority groups who hail this holding as their victory, they might consider the possible relevancy of this ancient remark: "Another such victory and I am undone."

Mr. Justice Douglas, dissenting.

. . . Debate and argument even in the courtroom are not always calm and dispassionate. Emotions sway speakers and audiences alike. Intemperate speech is a distinctive characteristic of man. Hot heads blow off and release destructive energy in the process. They shout and rave, exaggerating weaknesses, magnifying error, viewing with alarm. So it has been from the beginning; and so it will be throughout time. The Framers of the Constitution knew human nature as well as we do. They too had lived in dangerous days; they too knew the suffocating influence of orthodoxy and standardized thought. They weighed the compulsions for restrained speech and thought against the abuses of liberty. They chose liberty. That should be our choice today no matter how distasteful to us the pamphlet of Beauharnais may be. . . .

Mr. Justice Jackson, dissenting.

. . . Punishment of printed words, based on their *tendency* either to cause breach of the peace or injury to persons or groups, in my opinion, is justifiable only if the prosecution survives the "clear and present danger" test. . . .

One of the merits of the clear and present danger test is that the triers of fact would take into account the realities of race relations and any smouldering fires to be fanned into holocausts. Such consideration might well warrant a conviction here when it would not in another and different environment.

Group libel statutes represent a commendable desire to reduce sinister abuses of our freedom of expression. . . . I should be loath to foreclose the States from a considerable latitude of experimentation in this field. Such efforts, if properly applied, do not justify frenetic forebodings of crushed liberty. But these acts present most difficult policy and technical problems. . . .

No group interest in any particular prosecution should forget that the shoe may be on the other foot in some prosecution tomorrow. In these, as in other matters, our guiding spirit should be that each freedom is balanced with a responsibility, and every power of the State must be checked with safeguards. Such is the spirit of our American law of criminal libel, which concedes the power to the State, but only as a power restrained by recognition of individual rights. I cannot escape the conclusion that as the Act has been applied in this case it lost sight of the rights.

Mr. Justice Black's dissent evoked a heated attack from a critic who was inclined to place less value on free expression and more on public order.

Walter Berns:[18]

Beauharnais was not punished for anything he said, printed, or believed about the federal government, the state of Illinois, the city of Chicago, or any of their officials; the statute was not a sedition act. He was punished for what he said about other private citizens, over six hundred thousand

---

[18] Reprinted by permission of the publishers from Walter Berns, *Freedom, Virtue and the First Amendment*, pp. 152-54. Copyright © 1957 by the Louisiana State University Press.

of them. He was punished because he would deprive his fellow citizens of the equal protection of the laws. . . . But Black overlooks all this and sees the Illinois law as a state experiment in the curbing of freedom of expression and Beauharnais' petition as a "say in matters of public concern." The fact may be that this so-called "say" is the most imprudent and dangerous method of dealing with this matter of public concern. But as a Supreme Court justice he cannot even take such possibilities into consideration. . . .

It is hardly an exaggeration to say that to refer to Illinois' action against Beauharnais as an act of tyrannical government is to falsify the facts; at the very minimum, to do so is to miss something of the essence of the problem. The recent history of racial controversy . . . reveals problems whose solution requires judgment of a delicate sort. Chicago has more than its share of this controversy. Whatever might be said of the way the problem is handled by the city and state, it can scarcely be denied that leaflets of the sort Beauharnais circulated are not calculated to ameliorate it. On the contrary, the problem can only be exacerbated by publishing and distributing such things. Are these not facts that ought to be taken into consideration by the Court? Can any decision that ignores them be a just decision? But the libertarians can only see legislation of this sort as a "hobbling of political ideas."

As public officials they would not be unaware of the racial tension, and they would doubtless agree that appropriate measures be taken to alleviate it; but as Supreme Court justices they find this method to be prohibited by the Constitution. They are able to do this not because of some absolutely compelling terms in the Constitution (witness the majority that upheld the law) but because they regard all legislation of this type to be the acts of tyrants, promulgated to deprive Americans of their rightful liberties.

In all of the cases reviewed thus far where convictions had been obtained under licensing laws which the U. S. Supreme Court later found unconstitutional, defendants who had violated those laws were exonerated. It seemed taken for granted that an individual need not refrain from speaking because a public official had either denied him permission to do so or had not been asked for permission. However, in 1953, a majority of the Court took a somewhat different tack. The case concerned a Jehovah's Witness who had sought a license to conduct religious services in Portsmouth, New Hampshire's Goodwin Park. His application was denied; nevertheless he held his services in the park, was arrested, and convicted of violating the city's licensing requirement. Contrary to earlier cases of this kind, the U. S. Supreme Court agreed with the New Hampshire courts that the ordinance itself was a reasonable, nondiscriminatory regulation and hence constitutional, and that it had simply been misapplied by local authorities in this case. In other words, under the terms of the ordinance, a permit should have been issued. But, the Court went on, since the ordinance itself was valid, Poulos had no right to go ahead and speak without a license but should instead have resorted to judicial remedies to obtain one. Although this case differs from others we have considered, in that the ordinance itself was not found wanting, and the Court has in more recent years handed down decisions repetitive of earlier cases like Lovell and Thomas, the Poulos decision does create some uncertainties and hazards for the would-be violator of a licensing law.

POULOS v. NEW HAMPSHIRE [19]

Mr. Justice Reed delivered the opinion of the Court.

. . . The principles of the First Amendment are not to be treated as a promise that everyone with opinions or beliefs to express may gather around him at any public place and at any time a group for discussion or instruction. It is a *non sequitur* to say that First Amendment rights may not be regulated because they hold a preferred position in the hierarchy of the constitutional guarantees of the incidents of freedom. This Court has never so held and indeed has definitely indicated the contrary. It has indicated approval

[19] 345 US 395 (1953).

of reasonable nondiscriminatory regulation by governmental authority that preserves peace, order and tranquillity without deprivation of the First Amendment guarantees of free speech, press and the exercise of religion. When considering specifically the regulation of the use of public parks, this Court has taken the same position. . . . ordinances were held invalid, not because they regulated the use of the parks for meeting and instruction but because they left complete discretion to refuse in the hands of officials. . . . There is no basis for saying that freedom and order are not compatible. That would be a decision of desperation. Regulation and suppression are not the same, either in purpose or result, and courts of justice can tell the difference.

MR. JUSTICE BLACK, dissenting.

. . . I do not challenge the Court's argument that New Hampshire could prosecute a man who refused to follow the letter of the law to procure a license to "run businesses," "erect structure," "purchase firearms," "store explosives," or, I may add, to run a pawnshop. But the First Amendment affords freedom of speech a special protection; I believe it prohibits a state from convicting a man of crime whose only offense is that he makes an orderly religious appeal after he has been illegally, "arbitrarily and unreasonably" denied a "license" to talk. This to me is a subtle use of a creeping censorship loose in the land.

The name of George Lincoln Rockwell, leader of the American Nazi Party, is a familiar one around the country today. He has spoken in many cities and at many colleges, and has been banned at others. In May, 1960, Rockwell applied to the New York City Commissioner of Parks for a permit to speak on July 4 in Union Square. The request was denied without providing, as required by the ordinance, an offer of an alternative time and place. Rockwell went to court, asking that the commissioner be ordered to issue a permit. His petition was dismissed by the lower court, but the Appellate Division, in a 4-1 vote, reversed that decision and granted Rockwell's order.

ROCKWELL v. MORRIS [20]

BREITEL, Justice Presiding.

. . . A community need not wait to be subverted by street riots and stormtroopers; but, also, it cannot, by its policemen or commissioners, suppress a speaker, in prior restraint, on the basis of news reports, hysteria, or inference that what he did yesterday, he will do today. Thus, too, if the speaker incites others to immediate unlawful action he may be punished—in a proper case, stopped when disorder actually impends; but this is not to be confused with unlawful action from others who seek unlawfully to suppress or punish the speaker.

So, the unpopularity of their views, their shocking quality, their obnoxiousness, and even their alarming impact is not enough. Otherwise, the preacher of any strange doctrine could be stopped; the anti-racist himself could be suppressed, if he undertakes to speak in "restricted" areas; and one who asks that public schools be open indiscriminately to all ethnic groups could be lawfully suppressed, if only he choose to speak where persuasion is needed most.

. . . now, once again, against a speaker despised, hated, or feared, the lawless short-circuit is seized upon. The evil to be prevented provokes evil means to that end. This is not good law or good morals. No doubt, too, suppression is easier than punishment. No doubt suppressing a minority is easier than keeping a misbehaving majority in line. But that is exactly the purpose of law, and of government under law. . . .

Only if Rockwell speaks criminally (or, perhaps, if it is established on a proper record, in that very rare case, that he will speak criminally, not because he once did, but that he will this time, and irreparable harm will ensue) can his right to speak be cut off. If he does not speak criminally, then, of course, his right to speak may not be cut off, no matter how offensive his speech may be to others. Instead, his right, and that of those who wish to listen to him,

---

[20] 211 N.Y.S. 2d 25 (1961).

must be protected, no matter how unpleasant the assignment. . . .

Surely, there is risk in denying prior restraint. . . . But the risk is not so great as to be intolerable in a civilized, law-abiding community. Indeed, recent events, when especially provocative personalities attended an international meeting in this city, prove otherwise. Then these personalities did not represent mere mad ravings but effective, and not too remote, threats of widespread death and destruction. Nevertheless, the people, at least the residents, in this community, to many of whom these personalities were directly offensive and repugnant, did not resort to riot. They knew what was expected of them. It had also been made quite clear to them that the law was to be enforced without discrimination. The reward was not only the order which obtained, but the national respect that ensued for the people and their police force.

This decision was later affirmed without opinion by the New York Court of Appeals, and the U. S. Supreme Court declined a further hearing. Justice Breitel's view that audience hostility cannot be made the measure of a man's right to speak was also strongly reinforced by eight members of the U. S. Supreme Court two years later in a quite different context. A group of 187 Negro high school and college students had assembled on the state capitol grounds in Columbia, South Carolina, to make known their grievances to the members of the legislature. Upon disregarding a police order to disperse, they were arrested and convicted of the common law crime of a breach of the peace. The Supreme Court of South Carolina sustained their conviction, but only Justice Clark of the U. S. Supreme Court could agree with that decision.

EDWARDS v. SOUTH CAROLINA [21]

MR. JUSTICE STEWART delivered the opinion of the Court.

. . . it . . . remains our duty in a case such as this to

---

[21] 372 US 229 (1963).

make an independent examination of the whole record. . . . And it is clear to us that in arresting, convicting, and punishing the petitioners under the circumstances disclosed by this record, South Carolina infringed the petitioners' constitutionally protected rights of free speech, free assembly, and freedom to petition for redress of their grievances.

. . . The circumstances in this case reflect an exercise of these basic constitutional rights in their most pristine and classic form. The petitioners felt aggrieved by laws of South Carolina which allegedly "prohibited Negro privileges in this State." They peaceably assembled at the site of the State Government and there peaceably expressed their grievances "to the citizens of South Carolina, along with the Legislative Bodies of South Carolina." Not until they were told by police officials that they must disperse on pain of arrest did they do more. Even then, they but sang patriotic and religious songs after one of their leaders had delivered a "religious harangue." There was no violence or threat of violence on their part, or on the part of any member of the crowd watching them. Police protection was "ample."

This, therefore, was a far cry from the situation in *Feiner v. New York*. . . . And the record is barren of any evidence of "fighting words." . . . If . . . the petitioners had been convicted upon evidence that they had violated a law regulating traffic, or had disobeyed a law reasonably limiting the periods during which the State House grounds were open to the public, this would be a different case. . . . These petitioners were convicted of an offense so generalized as to be, in the words of the South Carolina Supreme Court, "not susceptible of exact definition." And they were convicted upon evidence which showed no more than that the opinions which they were peaceably expressing were sufficiently opposed to the views of the majority of the community to attract a crowd and necessitate police protection.

The Fourteenth Amendment does not permit a State to make criminal the peaceful expression of unpopular views. . . .

MR. JUSTICE CLARK, dissenting.

. . . The priceless character of First Amendment freedoms cannot be gainsaid, but it does not follow that they
are absolutes immune from necessary state action reasonably designed for the protection of society. . . . the petitioners were permitted without hindrance to exercise their
rights of free speech and assembly. Their arrests occurred
only after a situation arose in which the law-enforcement
officials on the scene considered that a dangerous disturbance was imminent. . . . in *Feiner* v. *New York* . . . we
upheld a conviction for breach of the peace in a situation
no more dangerous than that found here. There the demonstration was conducted by only one person and the
crowd was limited to approximately 80, as compared with
the present lineup of some 200 demonstrators and 300 on-
lookers. There . . . only one person—in a city having an
entirely different historical background—was exhorting
adults. Here 200 youthful Negro demonstrators were being
aroused to a "fever pitch" before a crowd of some 300
people who undoubtedly were hostile. Perhaps their speech
was not so animated but in this setting their actions, their
placards reading "You may jail our bodies but not our
souls" and their chanting of "I Shall Not Be Moved," accompanied by stamping feet and clapping hands, created a
much greater danger of riot and disorder. . . .

The gravity of the danger here surely needs no further
explication. . . . to say that the police may not intervene
until the riot has occurred is like keeping out the doctor
until the patient dies. I cannot subscribe to such a doctrine.

*It would appear, as of the present writing, that Justice
Clark's lone plea symbolizes the passing of an era in our
thinking about provocative speech, and that the position
of the American Civil Liberties Union, so often in the past
an opinion leader on First Amendment matters, points to
what the future will accept.*

American Civil Liberties Union:[22]

The Supreme Court has made it clear that the right of
assembly is a relative, not an absolute right. . . . But it
may be regulated only to protect substantial rights, not
merely to avoid inconvenience. . . . the right to assemble
and protest may not be denied to avoid possible public unrest, or even violent opposition. A permit may be required
for the holding of parades or public meetings, and meetings
and demonstrations may be regulated, for example to prevent undue restriction of normal traffic or to limit use of
facilities to one group at a time. But this power may not be
used to "protect" the public from exposure to what some
members of it—or some officials—do not want said.

. . . suggestions have been made by many of the highest
public authorities that assemblies likely to lead to breaches
of the peace should be avoided. . . . The point that has
not been made clear is that the important constitutional
right of protest cannot be abridged by the violent threats of
lawless individuals opposed to the objectives of the demonstrators.

The courts have plainly declared that important constitutional rights, such as free speech and assembly and equal
protection of the laws, cannot be curtailed because of apprehension that the exercise of these rights will result in
riotous disturbances by lawless opponents. The United
States Supreme Court very recently reiterated this point in
Wright v. *Georgia*, 373 US 284, in reversing the "breach
of peace" conviction of six Negroes for peacefully playing
basketball in a "whites only" public park. . . . In *Cooper*
v. *Aaron*, 358 US 1, the "lawless opponents" were state
officials themselves who . . . led the school authorities in
Little Rock, Arkansas, to ask a federal court to postpone
implementation of a desegregation plan because of extreme
public hostility. The Supreme Court rejected this petition
and ordered immediate reinstatement of the plan, saying

---

[22] Excerpts from "How Americans Protest." Statement of the American Civil Liberties Union, August, 1963.

that "law and order are not here to be preserved by depriving the Negro children of their constitutional rights."

. . . Means must be found to turn the forces of law and order to the protection of the demonstrators and to prevent violence by those who would attack them.

It is unthinkable that the constitutional right to demonstrate peaceably should be abridged by the least tolerant element in the community. . . .

Of course police may be compelled to stop a public meeting or demonstration if the situation develops to the point of imminent riot. But before the tension reaches that stage police must act to prevent hostile threats against peaceful demonstrators from being carried out and to arrest those seeking to break up an assembly.

QUESTIONS FOR DISCUSSION

1. Would the Cairo, Illinois, ordinance described at the opening of this chapter stand up under scrutiny by the U. S. Supreme Court?

2. What precedents might be cited as justification for the arrest and conviction of the Nazi pickets in front of the State-Lake Theatre in Chicago, also described at the opening of the chapter?

3. It can be argued that the Chaplinsky decision follows quite logically from what the Supreme Court said in Cantwell. It can also be argued that the two decisions are inconsistent with one another. How might each of these lines of argument be formulated?

4. On what basis might Justice Black have interpreted the Trenton loud-speaker ordinance in Kovacs as an absolute prohibition?

5. On what basis might one defend the opposite conclusions reached by the Court in the seemingly similar circumstances in Thomas and in Poulos?

6. What is meant by a permit ordinance which confers "ministerial rather than discretionary" power on the licensing official? Indicate cases which provide examples of each type.

7. What considerations appear to have influenced Justice Jackson in taking different directions in the Terminiello and Beauharnais cases?

8. In Edwards, Justices Stewart and Clark both make comparisons to the Feiner case. Which seems more persuasive? Might still another view be taken of the Feiner decision?

9. What similarities and what differences confronted the courts in the circumstances in the cases of Kunz and Rockwell?

10. Why would it not be possible, in circumstances such as those of Feiner or Terminiello, for the police simply to remove the speaker from the scene but bring no charges against him?

2

Political Heresy
and the
Problem of National Survival

---◆---

*"If there be any among us who wish to dissolve
this union, or to change its republican form, let
them stand undisturbed, as monuments of the
safety with which error of opinion may be tolerated where reason is left free to combat it."*
—Thomas Jefferson,
First Inaugural Address

A NORTH CAROLINA STORY

Colleges and universities, both public and private, across
the country have been the scene in recent years of innu-
merable conflicts over the banning by administrators of
controversial guest speakers invited to the campus by student groups. The list of speakers has included Nazi leader
George Lincoln Rockwell, Communist spokesman Herbert
Aptheker, and southern Governors George Wallace and
Ross Barnett. But in spite of these occasional bans, students have become increasingly active in seeking to hear
such speakers. Responding to this trend, the legislature of
the state of North Carolina, on June 26, 1963, during the
final hours of its 1963 session, operating under suspension
of the rules and without committee action, adopted an "act
to regulate visiting speakers at state-supported colleges and
universities." The act made it illegal for any college or uni-

versity which is supported by "any state funds" to "permit any person to use the facilities of such college or university for speaking purposes, who:

(A) Is a known member of the Communist Party;

(B) Is known to advocate the overthrow of the Constitution of the United States or the state of North Carolina;

(C) Has pleaded the Fifth Amendment of the Constitution of the United States in refusing to answer any question, with respect to communist or subversive connections. . . ."

The first application of this law occurred the following fall, when world-renowned British biologist J. B. S. Haldane was prohibited from lecturing at the University of North Carolina at Chapel Hill.

This action of the State of North Carolina denies the use of public facilities to a speaker on grounds quite different from those with which we have been concerned in the previous chapter. Here the question is not one of an immediate fight in the streets, but rather a fear that the ideas expressed may ultimately lead to an overturning of our basic political system. In this instance it has been a matter of prior restraint on the anticipated presentation of such views. But our country has also been involved, over the past fifty years, with an even greater number of cases in which advocates of political heresy, having spoken, have been arrested, convicted, and jailed.

Speech that is viewed with alarm by those who are satisfied with the norms under which they live is no doubt as ancient as organized society itself. Wherever groups have come together to form a social structure—be it a tribe, a city-state, a nation, or a religious institution—there have inevitably arisen dissidents so alienated from the mainstream of group life as to see no solution short of revolutionary change. This, of course, is viewed as a threat by those who value the survival of the structure, particularly if they sense that dissatisfaction in their ranks is sufficiently widespread that the spokesmen of revolt may find sympathetic ears. So arises the conflict—between those who seek to preserve themselves and the status quo through suppression of this heresy and those who either support the heretics or do not fear their tongues.

The Founding Fathers of the United States knew this kind of struggle from bitter personal experience. Many had themselves fled from political and religious suppression, and their new nation was born of revolution. But human beings sometimes forget or fail to understand fully the meaning of their own experiences. Thus some of these men, having established a society which they valued, became as aggressively protective of it as had the keepers of the societies against which they had rebelled. Religious sects that had grown from dissent became themselves intolerant and drove off dissenters. When the new nation faced one of its first major crises of criticism, the young Congress responded with the enactment of the Sedition Law of 1798 which provided that

> if any person shall write, print, utter, or publish . . . any false, scandalous and malicious writing or writings against the government . . . with intent to defame . . . or to bring . . . into contempt or disrepute; or to excite . . . the hatred of the good people of the United States . . . then such person . . . shall be punished by a fine not exceeding two thousand dollars, and by imprisonment not exceeding two years.

When Jefferson and his opposition party took office in 1801 the country turned its back on this legislation, and it was over a hundred years before the nation would again feel sufficiently threatened to enact such a law. This occurred when the stresses of domestic opposition to World War I and the influences of the Bolshevik revolution in Russia caused the Congress to embark on a series of measures designed to restrict antigovernment talk. First was the Espionage Act of 1917, which made it illegal to attempt to cause insubordination among the military services or to obstruct the draft. In 1918 this Act was amended to include several other offenses, among them saying anything designed to obstruct the sale of U. S. bonds or uttering any "disloyal, profane, scurrilous, or abusive language, or language intended to cause contempt, scorn, contumely or disrepute as regards the form of government of the United States." The 1918 amendment was repealed in 1921, but in 1940, in response to the continuing fear of Communist activity, the Alien Registration Act, sometimes known as the Smith Act, was passed. This bill makes it

unlawful for any person to knowingly or willfully advocate, abet, advise, or teach the duty, necessity, desirability, or propriety of overthrowing or destroying any government in the United States by force or violence

or to organize, help to organize, or become a member knowing its purposes of

any society, group, or assembly of persons who teach, advocate, or encourage the overthrow or destruction of any government in the United States by force or violence.

The Smith Act was supplemented in 1950 by the Subversive Activities Control Act, also known as the McCarran Act, which declares the Communist movement to be dedicated to the overthrow of the United States Government, orders that all Communist-action organizations must register data about their activities, officers, and membership with the Department of Justice, and subjects persons so registered to certain disabilities, such as denial of the opportunity for government employment.

These laws, plus others of similar nature at the state level directed at anarchy or criminal syndicalism as well as Communism, have been the source of many arrests and trials during this century in the United States. Out of the decisions in those cases, and the discussion of them, has emerged a body of doctrine governing the permissible scope of political heresy today. But many important issues still remain in dispute.

1. Should a society permit the advocacy of its own destruction?

2. At what point is it permissible to interfere with speech that might ultimately culminate in acts of revolu-

tion? Is the advocacy of revolution as an abstract idea
to be allowed? Is the advocacy of action, divorced from
the probability of any action immediately ensuing, to be
barred? Must a society, believing certain individuals to
be dedicated to its overthrow, wait to move against them
until guns are in their hands?

3. Is it possible or desirable to distinguish between
advocacy and incitement? Between a "speech-act" and
"mere speech"?

4. Shall the courts or our legislative bodies determine
what limits are to be set on the freedom of political dissent?

These are some of the problems to which the writers we
shall explore have addressed themselves.

―――――――――

The earliest case of significance under the Espionage Act
of 1917 arose when the postmaster of New York excluded
from the mails a revolutionary journal, The Masses, which
contained articles and cartoons attacking the war. Judge
Learned Hand of the U. S. District Court granted the publisher's request for an injunction against the postmaster's
action. After making clear that he did not regard all speech
as protected by the First Amendment, Judge Hand nevertheless rejected as a basis for suppression the mere possibility of indirect provocation to unlawful behavior. The
words themselves must be a direct incitement.

MASSES PUBLISHING CO. v. PATTEN [1]

JUDGE HAND:

. . . Words are not only the keys of persuasion, but the
triggers of action, and those which have no purport but to
counsel the violation of law cannot by any latitude of interpretation be a part of that public opinion which is the final
source of government in a democratic state. . . .

Political agitation, by the passions it arouses or the
convictions it engenders, may in fact stimulate men to the

―――――――――

[1] 244 Fed. 535 (S.D.N.Y., 1917).

violation of law. Detestation of existing policies is easily transformed into forcible resistance of the authority which puts them in execution, and it would be folly to disregard the causal relation between the two. Yet to assimilate agitation, legitimate as such, with direct incitement to violent resistance, is to disregard the tolerance of all methods of political agitation which in normal times is a safeguard of free government. The distinction is not a scholastic subterfuge, but a hard-bought acquisition in the fight for freedom.

Judge Hand's decision did not stand up on appeal, as is explained in the following analysis by Professor Chafee.

Zechariah Chafee, Jr.:[2]

. . . Judge Hand was reversed on a point of administrative law, that the postmaster's decision must stand unless clearly wrong; and, in addition, the Circuit Court of Appeals thought it desirable to reject his construction of the Espionage Act. . . . Judge Hand's objective test of the nature of the words was considered unsound. Advice in direct language was repudiated as a requisite of guilt. Judge Hough used the Sermon on the Mount as a precedent for the government's war policy: "It is at least arguable whether there can be any more direct incitement to action than to hold up to admiration those who do act. . . ." It is possible that the upper court did not intend to lay down a very different principle from Judge Hand, but chiefly wished to insist that in determining whether there is incitement one must look not only at the words themselves but also at the surrounding circumstances which may have given the words a special meaning to their hearers. Judge Hand agreed with this, and regarded Mark Antony's funeral oration, for instance, as having counseled violence while it expressly discountenanced it. However, the undoubted effect of the final decision in *Masses* v. *Patten* was

---

[2] Reprinted by permission of the publishers from Zechariah Chafee, Jr., *Free Speech in the United States* (Cambridge, Mass.: Harvard University Press), pp. 49-50. Copyright, 1941, by the President and Fellows of Harvard College.

to establish the old-time doctrine of remote bad tendency in the minds of district judges throughout the country.

———◆———

The first landmark decision of the U. S. Supreme Court in the field of political heresy was written in 1919 in response to an appeal by the general secretary of the Socialist Party, who had been convicted of violating the Espionage Act for sending leaflets to prospective military draftees urging them to resist the Conscription Act. In affirming his conviction, the Court enunciated the famous clear-and-present-danger formula for determining the limits of speech.

SCHENCK v. UNITED STATES [3]

MR. JUSTICE HOLMES delivered the opinion of the Court.

. . . The document would not have been sent unless it had been intended to have some effect, and we do not see what effect it could be expected to have upon persons subject to the draft except to influence them to obstruct the carrying of it out. . . . We admit that in many places and in ordinary times the defendants, in saying all that was said in the circular, would have been within their constitutional rights. But the character of every act depends upon the circumstances in which it is done. . . . The most stringent protection of free speech would not protect a man in falsely shouting fire in a theater, and causing a panic. It does not even protect a man from an injunction against uttering words that may have all the effect of force. . . . The question in every case is whether the words used are used in such circumstances and are of such a nature as to create a clear and present danger that they will bring about the substantive evils that Congress has a right to prevent. It is a question of proximity and degree. When a nation is at war many things that might be said in time of peace are such a hindrance to its effort that their utterance will not be endured so long as men fight, and that no Court could regard them as protected by any constitutional right.

---

[3] 249 US 47 (1919).

*In two ensuing decisions, Frohwerk v. United States, 249
US 204 (1919), and Debs v. United States, 249 US 211
(1919), Justice Holmes continued to believe that the
speech in question constituted a clear and present danger to
the war effort. But when the case of a left-wing pamphlet
that was directed only against the dispatch of U. S. troops to
Russia came before the Court, Justice Holmes, along with
Justice Brandeis, parted from the rest of his colleagues.
Holmes and Brandeis could no longer accept the seven-man
majority's broad view of what constituted forbidden communication.*

ABRAMS v. UNITED STATES [4]

MR. JUSTICE CLARKE delivered the opinion of the Court.

. . . It will not do to say . . . that the only intent of
these defendants was to prevent injury to the Russian
cause. Men must be held to have intended, and to be ac-
countable for, the effects which their acts were likely to
produce. Even if their primary purpose and intent was to
aid the cause of the Russian Revolution, the plan of action
which they adopted *necessarily* involved, before it could be
realized, defeat of the war program of the United States,
for the obvious effect of this appeal, if it should become
effective, as they hoped it might, would be to persuade persons . . . not to aid government loans and not to work in
ammunition factories. . . .

MR. JUSTICE HOLMES, dissenting.

This indictment is founded wholly upon the publication
of two leaflets. . . .

The first of these leaflets says that the President's cow-
ardly silence about the intervention in Russia reveals the
hypocrisy of the plutocratic gang in Washington. . . . It
says that there is only one enemy of the workers of the
world and that is capitalism; that it is a crime for workers
of America, etc., to fight the worker's republic of Russia,
and ends "Awake! Awake, you Workers of the World!
Revolutionists". . . .

The other leaflet, headed "Workers—Wake Up," with

---

[4] 250 US 616 (1919).

abusive language says that America together with the Allies will march for Russia to help the Czecho-Slovaks in their struggle against the Bolsheviki, and that this time the hypocrites shall not fool the Russian emigrants and friends of Russia in America. . . . The leaflet winds up by saying "Workers, our reply to this barbarous intervention has to be a general strike!" . . . "Woe unto those who will be in the way of progress. Let solidarity live! The Rebels."

. . . to make the conduct criminal . . . [the] statute requires that it should be "with intent by such curtailment to cripple or hinder the United States in the prosecution of the war." It seems to me that no such intent is proved.

. . . I never have seen any reason to doubt that the questions of law that alone were before this Court in the cases of *Schenck, Frohwerk* and *Debs,* . . . were rightly decided. . . . But . . . it is only the present danger of immediate evil or an intent to bring it about that warrants Congress in setting a limit to the expression of opinion. . . . An intent to prevent interference with the revolution in Russia might have been satisfied without any hindrance to carrying on the war in which we were engaged.

I do not see how anyone can find the intent required by the statute in any of the defendant's words. . . . To say that two phrases taken literally might import a suggestion of conduct that would have interference with the war as an indirect and probably undesired effect seems to me by no means enough to show an attempt to produce that effect.

. . . In this case sentences of twenty years imprisonment have been imposed for the publishing of two leaflets that I believe the defendants had as much right to publish as the Government has to publish the Constitution of the United States now vainly invoked by them. Even if I am technically wrong and enough can be squeezed from these poor and puny anonymities to turn the color of legal litmus paper; I will add, even if what I think the necessary intent were shown; the most nominal punishment seems to me all that possibly could be inflicted, unless the defendants are to be made to suffer not for what the indictment alleges but for the creed that they avow. . . .

Persecution for the expression of opinions seems to me perfectly logical. If you have no doubt of your premises or your power and want a certain result with all your heart you naturally express your wishes in law and sweep away all opposition. To allow opposition by speech seems to indicate that you think the speech impotent, as when a man says that he has squared the circle, or that you do not care whole-heartedly for the result, or that you doubt either your power or your premises. But when men have realized that time has upset many fighting faiths, they may come to believe even more than they believe the very foundations of their own conduct that the ultimate good desired is better reached by free trade in ideas—that the best test of truth is the power of the thought to get itself accepted in the competition of the market, and that truth is the only ground upon which their wishes safely can be carried out. That at any rate is the theory of our Constitution. It is an experiment, as all life is an experiment. Every year if not every day we have to wager our salvation upon some prophecy based upon imperfect knowledge. While that experiment is part of our system I think that we should be eternally vigilant against attempts to check the expression of opinions that we loathe and believe to be fraught with death, unless they so imminently threaten immediate interference with the lawful and pressing purposes of the law that an immediate check is required to save the country. I wholly disagree with the argument of the Government that the First Amendment left the common law as to seditious libel in force. History seems to me against the notion. I had conceived that the United States through many years had shown its repentance for the Sedition Act of 1798, by repaying fines that it imposed. Only the emergency that makes it immediately dangerous to leave the correction of evil counsels to time warrants making any exception to the sweeping command, "Congress shall make no law . . . abridging the freedom of speech." Of course I am speaking only of expressions of opinion and exhortations, which were all that were uttered here, but I regret that I cannot put into more impressive words my belief that in their conviction upon this indictment the defendants were deprived of their rights under the Constitution of the United States.

Another of the famed Holmes-Brandeis dissents occurred in 1925 in response to the Court's affirmation of the conviction of Benjamin Gitlow under a New York criminal anarchy statute. But the significance of this case goes far beyond their dissenting opinion. For the majority decision, while sustaining Gitlow's conviction, took a position, in justifying the Court's review of the case, that opened the way for all future free speech controversies to reach our highest court. The opinion declared explicitly for the first time that the prohibitions contained in the First Amendment against abridgments of free speech by the Federal Government were applicable to state governments as well, by virtue of the due process clause of the Fourteenth Amendment.

GITLOW v. NEW YORK [5]

Mr. Justice Sanford delivered the opinion of the Court.

Benjamin Gitlow was indicted in the supreme court of New York, with three others, for the statutory crime of criminal anarchy. . . .

The contention here is that the statute, by its terms and as applied in this case, is repugnant to the due process clause of the 14th Amendment. Its material provisions are: . . . Criminal anarchy is the doctrine that organized government should be overthrown by force or violence. . . . The advocacy of such doctrine either by word of mouth or writing is a felony. . . . The indictment . . . charged that the defendant had advocated, advised, and taught the duty, necessity, and propriety of overthrowing and overturning organized government by force, violence, and unlawful means, by certain writings therein set forth, entitled, "The Left Wing Manifesto." . . . The defendant is a member of the Left Wing section of the Socialist party, a dissenting branch or faction of that party, formed

---

[5] 268 US 652 (1925).

in opposition to its dominant policy of "moderate Socialism". . . . The sole contention here is, essentially, that, as
there was no evidence of any concrete result flowing from
the publication of the Manifesto, or of circumstances showing the likelihood of such result, the statute as construed
and applied by the trial court penalizes the mere utterance,
as such, of "doctrine" having no quality of incitement.
. . . The argument in support of this contention rests
primarily upon the following propositions: 1st, that the
"liberty" protected by the 14th Amendment includes the
liberty of speech and of the press; and 2d, that while
liberty of expression "is not absolute," it may be restrained
"only in circumstances where its exercise bears a causal
relation with some substantive evil, consummated, attempted, or likely;" and as the statute "takes no account
of circumstances," it unduly restrains this liberty, and is
therefore unconstitutional. . . .

The statute does not penalize the utterance or publication of abstract "doctrine" or academic discussion having
no quality of incitement to any concrete action. It is not
aimed against mere historical or philosophical essays. It
does not restrain the advocacy of changes in the form of
government by constitutional and lawful means. What it
prohibits is language advocating, advising, or teaching the
overthrow of organized government by unlawful means.
These words imply urging to action. . . .

The Manifesto, plainly, is neither the statement of abstract doctrine nor, as suggested by counsel, mere predic-
tion that industrial disturbances and revolutionary mass
strikes will result spontaneously in an inevitable process of
evolution in the economic system. It advocates and urges in
fervent language mass action which shall progressively fo-
ment industrial disturbances, and, through political mass
strikes and revolutionary mass action, overthrow and destroy organized parliamentary government. It concludes
with a call to action. . . .

For present purposes we may and do assume that freedom of speech and of the press—which are protected by
the First Amendment from abridgment by Congress—are
among the fundamental personal rights and "liberties" pro-

tected by the due process clause of the Fourteenth Amendment from impairment by the States. . . . That utterances inciting to the overthrow of organized government by unlawful means present a sufficient danger of substantive evil to bring their punishment within the range of legislative discretion is clear. Such utterances, by their very nature, involve danger to the public peace and to the security of the state. . . . And the immediate danger is none the less real and substantial because the effect of a given utterance cannot be accurately foreseen. The state cannot reasonably be required to measure the danger from every such utterance in the nice balance of a jeweler's scale. A single revolutionary spark may kindle a fire that, smoldering for a time, may burst into a sweeping and destructive conflagration. It cannot be said that the state is acting arbitrarily or unreasonably when, in the exercise of its judgment as to the measures necessary to protect the public peace and safety, it seeks to extinguish the spark without waiting until it has kindled the flame or blazed into the conflagration. . . . it may, in the exercise of its judgment, suppress the threatened danger in its incipiency. . . .

We cannot hold that the present statute is an arbitrary or unreasonable exercise of the police power of the state, unwarrantably infringing the freedom of speech or press; and we must and do sustain its constitutionality. . . .

Mr. Justice Holmes, dissenting.

Mr. Justice Brandeis and I are of the opinion that this judgment should be reversed. . . . I think that the criterion sanctioned by the full court in *Schenck* v. *United States* . . . applies. . . . It is true that in my opinion this criterion was departed from in *Abrams* v. *United States* . . . but the convictions that I expressed in that case are too deep for it to be possible for me as yet to believe that it and *Schaefer* v. *United States* . . . have settled the law. If what I think the correct test is applied, it is manifest that there was no present danger of an attempt to overthrow the government by force on the part of the admittedly small minority who shared the defendant's views. It is said that this Manifesto was more than a theory, that it was an incitement. Every idea is an incitement. It offers itself for belief,

and, if believed, it is acted on unless some other belief out-
weighs it, or some failure of energy stifles the movement
at its birth. The only difference between the expression of
an opinion and an incitement in the narrower sense is the
speaker's enthusiasm for the result. Eloquence may set fire
to reason. But whatever may be thought of the redundant
discourse before us, it had no chance of starting a present
conflagration. If, in the long run, the beliefs expressed in
proletarian dictatorship are destined to be accepted by the
dominant forces of the community, the only meaning of
free speech is that they should be given their chance and
have their way.

*The Gitlow opinions evoked this commentary by one of
our leading philosophers of free speech.*

Alexander Meiklejohn: [6]

Freedom to engage in "mere academic and harmless discussion"! Is that the freedom which is guarded by the First
Amendment? Is that the cause for which the followers of
Socrates have fought and died through the ages? As against
that intolerant belittling of the practical value of human
freedom of mind, Mr. Holmes, in his dissent, entered
spirited, if not very coherent, words of protest. . . .

Human discourse, as the First Amendment sees it, is not
"a mere academic and harmless discourse." If it were, the
advocates of self-government would be as little concerned
about it as they would be concerned about the freedom of
men playing solitaire or chess. The First Amendment was
not written primarily for the protection of those intellectual aristocrats who pursue knowledge solely for the fun of
the game. . . . It offers defense to men who plan and advocate and incite toward corporate action for the common
good.

———————————◆———————————

[6] Reprinted by permission of Harper & Row, Publishers, Inc., from
Alexander Meiklejohn, *Political Freedom*, pp. 41-42. Copyright © 1948,
1960 by Harper & Brothers.

Two years after Gitlow, Justice Brandeis delivered one of his *classic* statements on the rationale for freedom of speech. The occasion was a case from California in which Anita Whitney had been convicted of violating the state's criminal syndicalism act under circumstances that suggest that her "crime" was mere attendance at a radical convention. Because, in the trial, Miss Whitney did not make an issue of whether her activities constituted a clear and present danger, Justice Brandeis felt he had to concur in sustaining the action of the lower courts. But he proceeded nevertheless to make clear his views on the substance of the matter.

WHITNEY v. CALIFORNIA [7]

MR. JUSTICE BRANDEIS, concurring.

. . . This court has not yet fixed the standard by which to determine when a danger shall be deemed clear; how remote the danger may be and yet be deemed present; and what degree of evil shall be deemed sufficiently substantial to justify resort to abridgment of free speech and assembly as the means of protection. To reach sound conclusions on these matters, we must bear in mind why a state is, ordinarily, denied the power to prohibit dissemination of social, economic and political doctrine which a vast majority of citizens believes to be false and fraught with evil consequence.

Those who won our independence believed that the final end of the state was to make men free to develop their faculties; and that in its government the deliberative forces should prevail over the arbitrary. They valued liberty both as an end and as a means. They believed liberty to be the secret of happiness and courage to be the secret of liberty. They believed that freedom to think as you will and to speak as you think are means indispensable to the discovery and spread of political truth; that without free speech and assembly discussion would be futile; that with them, discussion affords ordinarily adequate protection against the dissemination of noxious doctrine; that the greatest menace to

---

[7] 274 US 357 (1927).

freedom is an inert people; that public discussion is a political duty; and that this should be a fundamental principle
of the American government. They recognized the risks to
which all human institutions are subject. But they knew
that order cannot be secured merely through fear of punishment for its infraction; that it is hazardous to discourage
thought, hope and imagination; that fear breeds repression;
that repression breeds hate; that hate menaces stable government; that the path of safety lies in the opportunity to
discuss freely supposed grievances and proposed remedies;
and that the fitting remedy for evil counsels is good ones.
Believing in the power of reason as applied through public
discussion, they eschewed silence coerced by law—the argument of force in its worst form. Recognizing the occasional tyrannies of governing majorities, they amended the
Constitution so that free speech and assembly should be
guaranteed.

Fear of serious injury cannot alone justify suppression of
free speech and assembly. Men feared witches and burned
women. It is the function of speech to free men from the
bondage of irrational fears. To justify suppression of free
speech there must be reasonable ground to fear that serious
evil will result if free speech is practiced. There must be
reasonable ground to believe that the danger apprehended
is imminent. There must be reasonable ground to believe
that the evil to be prevented is a serious one. Every denunciation of existing law tends in some measure to increase
the probability that there will be violation of it. Condona-
tion of a breach enhances the probability. Expressions of
approval add to the probability. Propagation of the criminal state of mind by teaching syndicalism increases it. Advocacy of lawbreaking heightens it still further. But even
advocacy of violation, however reprehensible morally, is not
a justification for denying free speech where the advocacy
falls short of incitement and there is nothing to indicate
that the advocacy would be immediately acted on. The
wide difference between advocacy and incitement, between
preparation and attempt, between assembling and conspiracy, must be borne in mind. In order to support a finding
of clear and present danger it must be shown either that

immediate serious violence was to be expected or was advocated, or that the past conduct furnished reason to believe that such advocacy was then contemplated.

Those who won our independence by revolution were not cowards. They did not fear political change. They did not exalt order at the cost of liberty. To courageous, self-reliant men, with confidence in the power of free and fearless reasoning applied through the processes of popular government, no danger flowing from speech can be deemed clear and present, unless the incidence of the evil apprehended is so imminent that it may befall before there is opportunity for full discussion. If there be time to expose through discussion the falsehood and fallacies, to avert the evil by the processes of education, the remedy to be applied is more speech, not enforced silence. Only an emergency can justify repression. Such must be the rule if authority is to be reconciled with freedom. Such, in my opinion, is the command of the Constitution. It is, therefore, always open to Americans to challenge a law abridging free speech and assembly by showing that there was no emergency justifying it.

Moreover, even imminent danger cannot justify resort to prohibition of these functions essential to effective democracy, unless the evil apprehended is relatively serious. Prohibition of free speech and assembly is a measure so stringent that it would be inappropriate as the means for averting a relatively trivial harm to society. A police measure may be unconstitutional merely because the remedy, although effective as means of protection, is unduly harsh or oppressive. Thus, a state might, in the exercise of its police power, make any trespass upon the land of another a crime, regardless of the results or of the intent or purpose of the trespasser. It might, also, punish an attempt, a conspiracy, or an incitement to commit the trespass. But it is hardly conceivable that this court would hold constitutional a statute which punished as a felony the mere voluntary assembly with a society formed to teach that pedestrians had the moral right to cross unenclosed, unposted, waste lands and to advocate their doing so, even if there was imminent danger that advocacy would lead to a trespass. The fact that speech is likely to result in some violence or in destruction of property is not enough to justify its suppression. There must be the probability of serious injury to the state. Among freemen, the deterrents ordinarily to be applied to prevent crime are education and punishment for violations of the law, not abridgment of the rights of free speech and assembly.

———————

If refusal to speak can be taken as the expression of a point of view, then an important case in the development of our free speech doctrine was one that arose when the Jehovah's Witnesses in West Virginia contested the right of public schools to compel their children to participate in pledging allegiance to the United States flag. In 1943 the Supreme Court found such coercion unconstitutional. In a dissenting opinion that passed no judgment on the wisdom of the flag salute requirement itself, Justice Frankfurter raised a warning which he was to repeat on many other occasions—that the Bill of Rights is on shaky foundations if we look to our courts rather than our legislators to forestall its erosion.

WEST VIRGINIA STATE BOARD OF EDUCATION v. BARNETTE [8]

Mr. Justice Jackson delivered the opinion of the Court. . . . The freedom asserted by these appellees does not bring them into collision with rights asserted by any other individuals. . . . the refusal of these persons to participate in the ceremony does not interfere with or deny rights of others to do so. . . . The sole conflict is between authority and rights of the individual. . . . we are dealing with a compulsion of students to declare a belief. They are not merely made acquainted with the flag salute so that they may be informed as to what it is or even what it means. The issue here is whether this slow and easily neglected route to aroused loyalties constitutionally may be short-cut by substituting a compulsory salute and slogan. . . .

———————

[8] 319 US 624 (1943).

There is no doubt that, in connection with the pledges, the flag salute is a form of utterance. Symbolism is a primitive but effective way of communicating ideas . . . a short cut from mind to mind. . . .

Over a decade ago Chief Justice Hughes led this court in holding that the display of a red flag as a symbol of opposition by peaceful and legal means to organized government was protected by the free speech guaranties of the Constitution. *Stromberg* v. *California* 283 US 359. . . . It is now a commonplace that censorship or suppression of expression of opinion is tolerated by our Constitution only when the expression presents a clear and present danger of action of a kind the State is empowered to prevent and punish. It would seem that involuntary affirmation could be commanded only on even more immediate and urgent grounds than silence. But here the power of compulsion is invoked without any allegation that remaining passive during a flag salute ritual creates a clear and present danger that would justify an effort even to muffle expression. To sustain the compulsory flag salute we are required to say that a Bill of Rights which guards the individual's right to speak his own mind, left it open to public authorities to compel him to utter what is not in his mind.

Whether the First Amendment to the Constitution will permit officials to order observance of ritual of this nature does not depend upon whether as a voluntary exercise we would think it to be good, bad or merely innocuous. . . .

Nor does the issue as we see it turn on one's possession of particular religious views or the sincerity with which they are held. While religion supplies appellees' motive for enduring the discomforts of making the issue in this case, many citizens who do not share these religious views hold such a compulsory rite to infringe constitutional liberty of the individual. . . .

Government of limited power need not be anemic government. . . . Without promise of a limiting Bill of Rights it is doubtful if our Constitution could have mustered enough strength to enable its ratification. To enforce those rights today is not to choose weak government over strong government. It is only to adhere as a means of strength to individual freedom of mind in preference to officially disciplined uniformity for which history indicates a disappointing and disastrous end. . . .

The Fourteenth Amendment, as now applied to the States, protects the citizen against the State itself and all of its creatures—Boards of Education not excepted. These have, of course, important, delicate, and highly discretionary functions, but none that they may not perform within the limits of the Bill of Rights. . . . There are village tyrants as well as village Hampdens, but none who acts under color of law is beyond reach of the Constitution. . . .

The very purpose of a Bill of Rights was to withdraw certain subjects from the vicissitudes of political controversy, to place them beyond the reach of majorities and officials and to establish them as legal principles to be applied by the courts. One's right to life, liberty, and property, to free speech, a free press, freedom of worship and assembly, and other fundamental rights may not be submitted to vote; they depend on the outcome of no elections. . . .

National unity as an end which officials may foster by persuasion and example is not in question. The problem is whether under our Constitution compulsion as here employed is a permissible means for its achievement.

Struggles to coerce uniformity of sentiment in support of some end thought essential to their time and country have been waged by many good as well as by evil men. . . . As governmental pressure toward unity becomes greater, so strife becomes more bitter as to whose unity it shall be. . . . Those who begin coercive elimination of dissent soon find themselves exterminating dissenters. Compulsory unification of opinion achieves only the unanimity of the graveyard.

It seems trite but necessary to say that the First Amendment to our Constitution was designed to avoid these ends by avoiding these beginnings. . . . Authority here is to be controlled by public opinion, not public opinion by authority. . . . To believe that patriotism will not flourish if patriotic ceremonies are voluntary and spontaneous instead of a compulsory routine is to make an unflattering estimate of the appeal of our institutions to free minds. . . .

If there is any fixed star in our constitutional constellation, it is that no official, high or petty, can prescribe what shall be orthodox in politics, nationalism, religion, or other matters of opinion or force citizens to confess by word or act their faith therein. If there are any circumstances which permit an exception, they do not now occur to us.

We think the action of the local authorities in compelling the flag salute and pledge transcends constitutional limitations on their power and invades the sphere of intellect and spirit which it is the purpose of the First Amendment to our Constitution to reserve from all official control.

Mr. Justice Frankfurter, dissenting.

. . . Of course patriotism cannot be enforced by the flag salute. But neither can the liberal spirit be enforced by judicial invalidation of illiberal legislation. Our constant preoccupation with the constitutionality of legislation rather than with its wisdom tends to preoccupation of the American mind with a false value. The tendency of focussing attention on constitutionality is to make constitutionality synonymous with wisdom, to regard a law as all right if it is constitutional. Such an attitude is a great enemy of liberalism. Particularly in legislation affecting freedom of thought and freedom of speech much which should offend a free-spirited society is constitutional. Reliance for the most precious interests of civilization, therefore, must be found outside of their vindication in courts of law. Only a persistent positive translation of the faith of a free society into the convictions and habits and actions of a community is the ultimate reliance against unabated temptations to fetter the human spirit.

The fear of revolutionary doctrine which produced the rash of free speech cases we have noted following World War I reached a peak once again in the aftermath of World War II and the renewal of tensions with the Soviet Union. The key case involved conviction under the Smith Act of

Eugene Dennis, secretary general of the Communist Party, and ten of his fellow Communist leaders, for advocating and conspiring to advocate forcible overthrow of our government. Judge Learned Hand, writing on behalf of the U. S. Second Circuit Court of Appeals, sustained the trial court's judgment.

UNITED STATES v. DENNIS [9]

JUDGE HAND:

. . . The question before us, and the only one, is how long a government, having discovered such a conspiracy, must wait. When does the conspiracy become a "present" danger. The jury has found that the conspirators will strike as soon as success seems possible. . . . Meanwhile they claim the constitutional privilege of going on indoctrinating their pupils . . . awaiting the moment when we may be so far extended by foreign engagements, so far divided in counsel, or so far in industrial or financial straits, that the chance seems worth trying. That position presupposes that the Amendment assures them freedom for all preparatory steps and in the end the choice of initiative. . . .

We need not say that even so thoroughly planned and so extensive a confederation would be a "present danger" at all times and in all circumstances; the question is how imminent: that is, how probable of execution—it was in the summer of 1948, when the indictment was found. We must not close our eyes to our position in the world at that time. . . . Any border fray, any diplomatic incident . . . might . . . lead to war. We do not understand how one could ask for a more probable danger. . . . The only justification that can be suggested is that in spite of their efforts to mask their purposes . . . discussion and publicity may so weaken their power that it will have ceased to be dangerous when the moment may come. That may be a proper enough antidote in ordinary times and for less redoubtable combinations; but certainly it does not apply to this one. . . . True, we must not forget our own faith; we must be sensitive to the dangers that lurk in any choice; but

---

[9] 183 F 2d 201 (2d Cir. 1950).

choose we must, and we shall be silly dupes if we forget that again and again in the past thirty years, just such preparations in other countries have aided to supplant existing governments, when the time was ripe. . . . We hold that it is a danger "clear and present."

The Dennis case was appealed to the U. S. Supreme Court, which sustained the conviction by a 6–2 majority. In so doing, the Chief Justice quoted and adopted in full Learned Hand's revised version of Holmes' clear-and-present-danger test. The implications of this revision seem to have been fully realized by the Court, for the majority opinion follows much the same line of reasoning as that set forth by Justice Sanford in Gitlow—that when speech contains a tendency toward revolution it is foolish not to stop it in its initial stage. Justices Black and Douglas, too, were fully aware of the far-reaching implications of the decision, and raised their voices in vigorous protest.

DENNIS v. UNITED STATES [10]

MR. CHIEF JUSTICE VINSON delivered the opinion of the Court.

. . . Whatever theoretical merit there may be to the argument that there is a "right" to rebellion against dictatorial governments is without force where the existing structure of government provides for peaceful and orderly change. We reject any principle of governmental helplessness in the face of preparation for revolution, which principle, carried to its logical conclusion, must lead to anarchy. . . . the Smith Act . . . is directed at advocacy, not discussion. Thus, the trial judge properly charged the jury that they could not convict if they found that petitioners did "no more than pursue peaceful studies and discussions or teaching and advocacy in the realm of ideas". . . . where an offense is specified by a statute in nonspeech or nonpress terms, a conviction relying upon speech or press as evidence of violation may be sustained only when the speech or publication created a "clear and present danger"

---

[10] 341 US 494 (1951).

of attempting or accomplishing the prohibited crime. . . .
To those who would paralyze our Government in the face
of impending threat by encasing it in a semantic strait-
jacket we must reply that all concepts are relative.

. . . In this case we are squarely presented with the application of the "clear and present danger" test, and must
decide what that phrase imports. . . . Obviously, the words
cannot mean that before the Government may act, it
must wait until the *putsch* is about to be executed, the
plans have been laid and the signal is awaited. . . . Certainly an attempt to overthrow the Government by force,
even though doomed from the outset because of inadequate numbers or power of the revolutionists, is a sufficient
evil for Congress to prevent. The damage which such attempts create both physically and politically to a nation
makes it impossible to measure the validity in terms of the
probability of success, or the immediacy of a successful attempt. . . . We must therefore reject the contention that
success or probability of success is the criterion.

. . . Chief Judge Learned Hand . . . interpreted the
phrase as follows: "In each case [courts] must ask whether
the gravity of the 'evil,' discounted by its improbability,
justifies such invasion of free speech as is necessary to avoid
the danger". . . . We adopt this statement of the rule. As
articulated by Chief Judge Hand, it is as succinct and in-
clusive as any other we might devise at this time. It takes
into consideration those factors which we deem relevant,
and relates their significance. More we cannot expect from
words.

. . . Likewise, we are in accord with the court below,
which affirmed the trial court's finding that the requisite
danger existed. . . . If the ingredients of the reaction are
present, we cannot bind the Government to wait until the
catalyst is added.

. . . The judgments of conviction are affirmed.

Mr. Justice Frankfurter, concurring.

. . . The language of the First Amendment is to be read
not as barren words found in a dictionary but as symbols
of historic experience illumined by the presuppositions of
those who employed them. . . . Absolute rules would in-

evitably lead to absolute exceptions, and such exceptions would eventually corrode the rules. The demands of free speech in a democratic society as well as the interest in national security are better served by candid and informed weighing of the competing interests, within the confines of the judicial process, than by announcing dogmas too inflexible for the non-Euclidean problems to be solved.

. . . Free-speech cases are not an exception to the principle that we are not legislators, that direct policy-making is not our province. How best to reconcile competing interests is the business of legislatures, and the balance they strike is a judgment not to be displaced by ours, but to be respected unless outside the pale of fair judgment.

. . . No matter how rapidly we utter the phrase "clear and present danger," or how closely we hyphenate the words, they are not a substitute for the weighing of values.

. . . The defendants have been convicted of conspiring to organize a party of persons who advocate the overthrow of the Government by force and violence. The jury has found that the object of the conspiracy is advocacy as "a rule or principle of action," "by language reasonably and ordinarily calculated to incite persons to such action," and with the intent to cause the overthrow "as speedily as circumstances would permit."

On any scale of values which we have hitherto recognized, speech of this sort ranks low. . . .

It is true that there is no divining rod by which we may locate "advocacy." Exposition of ideas readily merges into advocacy. The same Justice who gave currency to application of the incitement doctrine in this field dissented four times from what he thought was its misapplication. As he said in the *Gitlow* dissent, "Every idea is an incitement." . . .

But there is underlying validity in the distinction between advocacy and the interchange of ideas, and we do not discard a useful tool because it may be misused. That such a distinction could be used unreasonably by those in power against hostile or unorthodox views does not negate the fact that it may be used reasonably against an organization wielding the power of the centrally controlled interna-

tional Communist movement. The object of the conspiracy
before us is clear enough that the chance of error in saying
that the defendants conspired to advocate rather than to
express ideas is slight. Mr. Justice Douglas quite properly
points out that the conspiracy before us is not a conspiracy
to overthrow the Government. But it would be equally wrong
to treat it as a seminar in political theory.

Mr. Justice Black, dissenting.

. . . At the outset I want to emphasize what the crime
involved in this case is, and what it is not. These petitioners
were not charged with an attempt to overthrow the Government. They were not charged with overt acts of any
kind designed to overthrow the Government. They were
not even charged with saying anything or writing anything
designed to overthrow the Government. The charge was
that they agreed to assemble and to talk and publish certain ideas at a later date. . . . No matter how it is worded,
this is a virulent form of prior censorship of speech and
press, which I believe the First Amendment forbids. . . .

So long as this Court exercises the power of judicial review of legislation, I cannot agree that the First Amendment permits us to sustain laws suppressing freedom of
speech and press on the basis of Congress' or our own notions of mere "reasonableness." Such a doctrine waters
down the First Amendment so that it amounts to little
more than an admonition to Congress. The Amendment as
so construed is not likely to protect any but those "safe" or
orthodox views which rarely need its protection.

Mr. Justice Douglas, dissenting.

If this were a case where those who claimed protection
under the First Amendment were teaching the techniques
of sabotage, the assassination of the President, the filching
of documents from public files, the planting of bombs, the
art of street warfare, and the like, I would have no
doubts. . . . This case was argued as if those were the
facts. . . . But the fact is that no such evidence was introduced at the trial. There is a statute which makes a seditious conspiracy unlawful. Petitioners, however, were not
charged with a "conspiracy to overthrow" the Government.
They were charged with a conspiracy to form a party and

groups and assemblies of people who teach and advocate the overthrow of our Government by force or violence and with a conspiracy to advocate and teach its overthrow by force and violence. . . .

So far as the present record is concerned, what petitioners did was to organize people to teach and themselves teach the Marxist-Leninist doctrine contained chiefly in four books. . . . But if the books themselves are not outlawed, if they can lawfully remain on library shelves, by what reasoning does their use in a classroom become a crime? . . . The Act, as construed, requires the element of intent—that those who teach the creed believe in it. The crime then depends not on what is taught but on who the teacher is. That is to make freedom of speech turn not on *what is said*, but on the *intent* with which it is said. Once we start down that road we enter territory dangerous to the liberties of every citizen.

There was a time in England when the concept of constructive treason flourished. Men were punished not for raising a hand against the king but for thinking murderous thoughts about him. The Framers of the Constitution were alive to that abuse and took steps to see that the practice would not flourish here. Treason was defined to require overt acts. . . . The present case is not one of treason. But the analogy is close when the illegality is made to turn on intent, not on the nature of the act. We then start probing men's minds for motive and purpose; they become entangled in the law not for what they did but *for what they thought*; they get convicted not for what they said but for the purpose with which they said it.

. . . I repeat that we deal here with speech alone, not with speech *plus* acts of sabotage or unlawful conduct. Not a single seditious act is charged in the indictment. . . .

The nature of Communism as a force on the world scene would, of course, be relevant to the issue of clear and present danger of petitioner's advocacy within the United States. But the primary consideration is the strength and tactical position of petitioners and their converts in this country. On that there is no evidence in the record. . . .

How it can be said that there is a clear and present danger that this advocacy will succeed is, therefore, a mystery. Some nations less resilient than the United States, where illiteracy is high and where democratic traditions are only budding, might have to take drastic steps and jail these men for merely speaking their creed. But in America they are miserable merchants of unwanted ideas; their wares remain unsold. The fact that their ideas are abhorrent does not make them powerful.

. . . Free speech—the glory of our system of government—should not be sacrificed on anything less than plain and objective proof of danger that the evil advocated is imminent. . . . This does not mean, however, that the Nation need hold its hand until it is in such weakened condition that there is no time to protect itself from incitement to revolution. Seditious conduct can always be punished. . . . The First Amendment reflects the philosophy of Jefferson "that it is time enough for the rightful purposes of civil government for its officers to interfere when principles break out into overt acts against peace and good order."

The Dennis decision, for all its length, settled matters for only six years. And then the tenuous line the Court majority had tried to draw between "discussion" and "advocacy" returned to plague them once again. A new case, involving fourteen more Communist Party leaders also convicted under the Smith Act, came up on appeal. But this time the connection between the speech of the defendants and potential revolutionary results seemed more remote than in Dennis. The high court slapped the wrist of the District Judge for failing to see this distinction and for misunderstanding its Dennis prose. As if aware, however, that the fault may have lain in the writing rather than the reading, Justice Harlan tried again to elucidate the difference—this time phrasing it not as a distinction between discussion and advocacy, but rather between advocacy of abstract doctrine, which is permissible, and advocacy of action, which is not. Because the lower court had failed to grasp this subtle difference, the convictions were reversed.

YATES v. UNITED STATES [11]

MR. JUSTICE HARLAN delivered the opinion of the Court.
. . . The distinction between advocacy of abstract doctrine and advocacy directed at promoting unlawful action is one that has been consistently recognized in the opinions of this Court. . . . The legislative history of the Smith Act and related bills shows beyond all question that Congress was aware of the distinction between the advocacy or teaching of abstract doctrine and the advocacy or teaching of action, and that it did not intend to disregard it. The statute was aimed at the advocacy and teaching of concrete action for the forcible overthrow of the Government, and not of principles divorced from action. . . .

In failing to distinguish between advocacy of forcible overthrow as an abstract doctrine and advocacy of action to that end, the District Court appears to have been led astray by the holding in *Dennis* that advocacy of violent action to be taken at some future time was enough. It seems to have considered that, since "inciting" speech is usually thought of as calculated to induce immediate action, and since *Dennis* held advocacy of action for future overthrow sufficient, this meant that advocacy, irrespective of its tendency to generate action, is punishable, provided only that it is uttered with a specific intent to accomplish overthrow. . . .

This misconceives the situation confronting the Court in *Dennis* and what was held there. . . . The essential distinction is that those to whom the advocacy is addressed must be urged to *do* something, now or in the future, rather than merely to *believe* in something. At best the expressions used by the trial court were equivocal. . . .

We recognize that distinctions between advocacy or teaching of abstract doctrines, with evil intent, and that which is directed to stirring people to action, are often subtle and difficult to grasp. . . . But the very subtlety of these distinctions required the most clear and explicit in-

---

[11] 354 US 298 (1957).

structions with reference to them, for they concerned an issue which went to the very heart of the charges against these petitioners.

Lest we think that the Yates decision has provided a definitive solution to the problem of distinguishing satisfactorily between permissible and forbidden advocacy, let us turn to a brief comment on the matter by a legal scholar made in another context many years ago.

Francis Wharton:[12]

. . . Lord Chesterfield, in his letters to his son, directly advises the latter to form illicit connections with married women; Lord Chesterfield, on the reasoning here contested, would be indictable for solicitation to adultery. . . . to make bare solicitations or allurements indictable as *attempts*, not only unduly and perilously extends the scope of penal adjudication, but forces on the courts psychological questions which they are incompetent to decide, and a branch of business which would make them despots of every intellect in the land.

It was ten years after the Dennis decision before the question of membership, as opposed to leadership, in the Communist Party came before the U. S. Supreme Court. Three opinions, handed down on the same day, dealt with various aspects of this problem. The first, Communist Party v. Subversive Activities Control Board, 367 US 1 (1961), sustained a government order under the 1950 McCarran Act requiring the Commnist Party to register as a subversive organization. To the majority this decision affirmed what was to them merely a regulatory, not a punitive law. To the four-man minority its actual effect, combined with the 1940 Smith Act, was to incriminate all Communist Party members.

The other two decisions dealt with convictions of individ-

---

[12] From *Criminal Law*, 2d Ed, I, 179.

ual Communists, Junius Scales and John Noto, for violation of that clause of the Smith Act making illegal "knowing membership" in an organization dedicated to the violent overthrow of government. The Court took the position in these cases that, in order to be punished, one's membership in the Communist Party must be "active," and evidence must be presented of the advocacy of revolutionary action rather than abstract revolutionary doctrine. On these grounds, Noto's conviction was unanimously reversed, *Noto v. United States*, 367 US 290, but that of Scales was affirmed by a 5–4 vote. The Scales minority of four was the same as that in the Communist Party registration case and, indeed, as that in another crucial series of free speech cases we shall examine shortly—Justices Black, Douglas, Brennan, and Chief Justice Warren. The philosophy which motivated this minority was perhaps epitomized by Mr. Justice Douglas in his Scales dissent.

SCALES v. UNITED STATES [13]

MR. JUSTICE DOUGLAS, dissenting.

. . . Even the Alien and Sedition Laws—shameful reminders of an early chapter in intolerance—never went so far as we go today. They were aimed at conspiracy and advocacy of insurrection. . . . There is here no charge of conspiracy, no charge of any overt act to overthrow the Government by force and violence, no charge of any other criminal act. . . .

We legalize today guilt by association, sending a man to prison when he committed no unlawful act. . . .

The case is not saved by showing that petitioner was an active member. None of the activity constitutes a crime. . . .

Of course, government can move against those who take up arms against it. Of course, the constituted authority has the right of self-preservation. But we deal in this prosecution of Scales only with the legality of ideas and beliefs, not with overt acts. . . .

What we lose by majority vote today may be reclaimed

---

[13] 367 US 203 (1961).

at a future time when the fear of advocacy, dissent, and nonconformity no longer cast a shadow over us.

———◆———

An arena in which some of the most significant conflicts of our time have been fought over the government's efforts to preserve itself against the alleged dangers of political heresy has been the hearing room of the Committee on Un-American Activities of the U. S. House of Representatives (often referred to as HUAC). This committee, which was authorized by its parent body to investigate "the extent, character, and objects of un-American propaganda activities in the United States," has run headlong into the vigorously advocated contention that to pursue such a goal is to violate the First Amendment freedoms of speech and association of those whom the Committee calls before it for questioning. Although much of the publicity surrounding the committee's work has centered on witnesses who have claimed the Fifth Amendment privilege against self-incrimination, the most interesting cases from our point of view are those where the First Amendment has been used as a basis for refusing to answer questions.

In 1957, six justices of the U. S. Supreme Court agreed that a contempt of Congress conviction for refusing to answer HUAC's questions could not stand because the committee had failed to show the relevancy of its questions to a valid legislative inquiry (Watkins v. United States, 354 US 178). The same six justices also held that a guest lecturer at the University of New Hampshire need not respond to investigatory questions concerning his lectures put to him by that state's attorney general (Sweezy v. New Hampshire, 354 US 234). Thus it appeared that the whistle had been blown on government attempts to probe into the political activities of citizens.

But, in 1959, the Court sharply changed direction in the case of Barenblatt v. United States, 360 US 109. Lloyd Barenblatt was a young psychology professor at Vassar College who had been summoned before HUAC in 1954 and had refused to answer questions on First Amendment grounds. He was convicted of contempt and his appeal was rejected. *Justice Harlan, writing for a five-man majority, declared that:*

> . . . the protections of the First Amendment . . . do not afford a witness the right to resist inquiry in all circumstances. Where First Amendment rights are asserted to bar governmental interrogation resolution of the issue always involves a balancing by the courts of the competing private and public interests at stake in the particular circumstances shown. . . . We conclude that the balance between the individual and the governmental interests here at stake must be struck in favor of the latter, and that therefore the provisions of the First Amendment have not been offended.

Justices Black, Brennan, Douglas, and Chief Justice Warren dissented vehemently, as they were to do twice again in comparable circumstances in 1961 (Wilkinson v. United States, 365 US 399, and Braden v. United States, 365 US 431). Said Justice Black of the majority's Barenblatt opinion:

> Such a balance . . . completely leaves out the real interest in Barenblatt's silence, the interest of the people as a whole in being able to join organizations, advocate causes and make political "mistakes" without later being subjected to governmental penalties for having dared to think for themselves.

Meanwhile, repeated efforts in the Congress itself to abolish HUAC or to cut its budget have been unable to muster the votes of more than a handful of hardy representatives.

Contempt of Congress by refusal to discuss one's political ideology or associations in response to committee investigations has thus taken its place alongside punishment for the advocacy of overthrow of government as a limitation on First Amendment freedoms now sanctioned by our courts. But the judiciary has, in this respect, been more generous with legislators' assertions of authority over those who defy them than with the officers of its own establishment or of the executive branches of government.

We found in Near v. Minnesota that so-called libel against local administrative officials could not be restrained. In 1941, in Bridges v. California, 314 US 252, the U. S. Supreme Court handed down the first of a series of decisions overturning contempt of court convictions for criticism of the conduct of judges. Speaking for the Court, Mr. Justice Black said, "It is a prized American privilege to speak one's mind, although not always with perfect good taste, on all public institutions."

Then, in 1960, there appeared a signed advertisement in The New York Times criticizing the government of the city of Montgomery, Alabama, for its cruel mishandling of civil rights demonstrations. On the basis of some factual errors in the statement and alleged defamation, City Commissioner L. B. Sullivan sued The New York Times and four authors of the advertisement for libel. The Alabama courts awarded damages of half a million dollars, but were overruled by a unanimous U. S. Supreme Court.

NEW YORK TIMES CO. v. SULLIVAN [14]

MR. JUSTICE BRENNAN delivered the opinion of the Court.

We are required for the first time in this case to determine the extent to which the constitutional protections for speech and press limit a state's power to award damages in a libel action brought by a public official against critics of his official conduct. . . .

Respondent relies heavily, as did the Alabama courts, on statements of this court to the effect that the Constitution does not protect libelous publications.

Those statements do not foreclose our inquiry here. None of the cases sustained the use of libel laws to impose sanctions upon expression critical of the official conduct of public officials. . . . In deciding the question now, we are compelled by neither precedent nor policy to give any more weight to the epithet "libel" than we have to other "mere labels" of state law. . . . Like "insurrection," contempt, advocacy of unlawful act, breach of the peace, obscenity,

[14] 376 US 254 (1964).

solicitation of legal business and the various other formulae for the repression of expression that have been challenged in this court, libel can claim no talismanic immunity from constitutional limitations. It must be measured by standards that satisfy the First Amendment. . . . we consider this case against the background of a profound national commitment to the principle that debate on public issues should be uninhibited, robust, and wide open, and that it may well include vehement, caustic, and sometimes unpleasantly sharp attacks on government and public officials. . . . The present advertisement, as an expression of grievance and protest on one of the major public issues of our time, would seem clearly to qualify for the constitutional protection. The question is whether it forfeits that protection by the falsity of some of its factual statements and by its alleged defamation of respondent.

Authoritative interpretations of the First Amendment guarantees have consistently refused to recognize an exception for any test of truth, whether administered by judges, juries, or administrative officials—and especially not one that puts the burden of proving truth on the speaker. . . .

Just as a factual error affords no warrant for repressing speech that would otherwise be free, the same is true of injury to official reputation. Where judicial officers are involved . . . repression can be justified, if at all, only by a clear and present danger of the obstruction of justice. . . . If neither factual error nor defamatory content suffices to remove the constitutional shield from criticism of official conduct, the combination of the two elements is no less inadequate. This is the lesson to be drawn from the great controversy over the Sedition Act of 1798. . . . Although the Sedition Act was never tested in this court, the attack upon its validity has carried the day in the court of history. Fines levied in its prosecution were repaid by Act of Congress on the ground that it was unconstitutional. . . . Jefferson, as President, pardoned those who had been convicted and sentenced. . . . The invalidity of the act has also been assumed by justices of this court. . . .

There is no force in respondent's argument that the constitutional limitations implicit in the history of the Sedition

Act apply only to Congress and not to the states. It is true that the First Amendment was originally addressed only to action by the Federal Government, and that Jefferson, for one, while denying the power of Congress "to control the freedom of the press," recognized such a power in the states. . . . But this distinction was eliminated with the adoption of the 14th Amendment and the application to the states of the First Amendment's restrictions. . . .

Allowance of the defense of truth, with the burden of proving it on the defendant, does not mean that only false speech will be deterred. . . . Under such a rule, would-be critics of official conduct may be deterred from voicing their criticism, even though it is believed to be true and even though it is in fact true, because of doubt whether it can be proved in court or fear of the expense of having to do so. They tend to make only statements which "steer far wider of the unlawful zone". . . .

The constitutional guarantees require, we think, a Federal rule that prohibits a public official from recovering damages for a defamatory falsehood relating to his official conduct unless he proves that the statement was made with "actual malice"—that is, with knowledge that it was false or with reckless disregard of whether it was false or not.

Mr. Justice Goldberg with whom Mr. Justice Douglas joins, concurring in the result.

. . . In my view, the First and Fourteenth Amendments to the Constitution afford to the citizen and to the press an absolute, unconditional privilege to criticize official conduct. . . . The right should not depend upon a probing by the jury of the motivation of the citizen or press. The theory of our Constitution is that every citizen may speak his mind and every newspaper express its view on matters of public concern and may not be barred from speaking or publishing because those in control of government think that what is said or written is unwise, unfair, false, or malicious. . . . It has been recognized that "prosecutions for libel on government have (no) place in the American system of jurisprudence," *City of Chicago* v. *Tribune Co.* . . . I fully agree. Government, however, is not an abstraction; it is made up of individuals. . . . If the rule

that libel on government has no place in our Constitution
is to have real meaning, then libel on the official conduct of
the governors likewise can have no place in our Constitution. . . . It may be urged that deliberately and maliciously false statements have no conceivable value as free
speech. That argument, however, is not responsive to the
real issue presented by this case, which is whether that freedom of speech which all agree is constitutionally protected
can be effectively safeguarded by a rule allowing the imposition of liability upon a jury's evaluation of the speaker's
state of mind.

If individual citizens may be held liable in damages for
strong words, which a jury finds false and maliciously motivated, there can be little doubt that public debate and advocacy will be constrained.

There are two points of particular interest in this most
recent Supreme Court pronouncement on freedom of
speech. The first is Justice Brennan's suggestion, which
could have vast portent for the future, that the Court may
find a way to define back into the protections of the First
Amendment those areas of speech such as libel and obscenity which Chaplinsky and Beauharnais carved out of it.
The other is that in excepting "reckless" and "malicious"
libel of public officials from First Amendment protection,
the Court, as Justices Goldberg and Douglas noted, in
granting a seeming victory to freedom of expression in this
case, may actually have established a more restrictive
standard than had heretofore been assumed. This, indeed,
became clearer in November, 1964, in another case involving alleged criminal defamation of public officials (Garrison
v. Louisiana, 379 US 64), when Justice Brennan wrote for
the court:

Although honest utterance, even if inaccurate, may
further the fruitful exercise of the right of free speech,
it does not follow that the lie, knowingly and deliberately published about a public official, should enjoy a
like immunity. At the time the First Amendment was
adopted, as today, there were those unscrupulous

enough and skillful enough to use the deliberate or
reckless falsehood as an effective political tool to un-
seat the public servant or even topple an administration. That speech is used as a tool for political ends
does not automatically bring it under the protective
mantle of the constitution. For the use of the known
lie as a tool is at once at odds with the premises of
democratic government and with the orderly manner
in which economic, social, or political change is to be
effected. Calculated falsehood falls into that class of
utterances which "are no essential part of any exposition of ideas . . ."

*In this particular case the Supreme Court found insufficient
proof of calculated falsehood and overturned Garrison's conviction, but the way is clearly open for convictions in the
future under this standard.*

◆

We have seen where the law of the land, enacted by
Congress and interpreted by the Supreme Court, now
stands with regard to political heresy and criticism.
Whether this is where it should stand is another question,
open to philosophers and laymen as well as legislators and
judges. Let us first turn, then, to some of the arguments of
those who oppose the suppression of revolutionary talk.

Swineburne Hale:[15]

That . . ."Reds" in arguing their program should occasionally use loose and violent language is inevitable. Political talk is likely to be excited talk, as witness the remark of
that conservative of conservatives, Senator Fall, in debating
the Treaty with Senator Hitchcock: "God deliver us from
the necessity of appealing to the ultimate powers of the
people of the United States to change forcibly their form
of government!"—or the remark of that other arch-
conservative, Secretary of State Langtry of Massachusetts,

[15] Reprinted from Swineburne Hale, "The 'Force and Violence' Joker,"
The New Republic (January 21, 1920), p. 232.

speaking in a Church of God the other day on American "Bolshevists" and "traitors": "If I had my way I would take them out in the yard every morning and shoot them, and the next day would have a trial to see whether they were guilty." Now as a matter of fact Senator Fall would not dream of appealing to force to change the government, nor would Secretary Langtry think of raising a pistol against a real Red who stood before him in shabby clothing in his front yard. Such talk is simply political violence, excited and overstated, because of extreme conviction and deep feeling. We do not propose to put such people in jail—and quite rightly. Why? Because they are not, as a fact, inciting to violence. They are not urging anybody in particular, or even people in general, to commit the crimes indicated. They are simply blowing off pressure of overheated political ideas, and we rely on the good sense of everybody not to take them too seriously. To jail them for such explosions would be like jailing one's motor tire because it had blown out. It is the nature of tires and men to blow out under unusual circumstances; it is also their nature not to do so most of the time, and not really to intend to do so at any time.

Zechariah Chafee, Jr.:[16]

The normal law, which refrains from punishing words for their bad political tendency, has carried us through far worse crises than the period following the armistice. In the midst of the great railroad strikes of 1877, when unemployment was very large, a big communist meeting was permitted in New York. The Seventh Regiment was kept in a conspicuous readiness to put down any actual disorder, but there was no interference with anything that was said. The speakers indulged in the wildest kind of talk, but it fell flat on the meeting just because there was no chance for a row. Arthur Woods used the same wise policy when he became

---

[16] Reprinted by permission of the publishers from Zechariah Chafee, Jr., *Free Speech in the United States* (Cambridge, Mass.: Harvard University Press), pp. 156, 178-94. Copyright, 1941, by the President and Fellows of Harvard College.

police commissioner of New York City during the hard times of the summer of 1914. Under his predecessor the police had been breaking up anarchistic meetings in Union Square every Saturday afternoon. . . . Mr. Woods took office, and told the police to interfere in any actual disturbance, but not otherwise. . . . Mr. Woods says:

> The change of method was almost unbelievably successful. There was no disorder; the crowd was very large but very well behaved, and at the end of the meeting when everything was over and many had gone home, three cheers were proposed and given for the police.

We ought to disagree vehemently with those who urge violent methods, and whenever necessary take energetic steps to prevent them from putting such methods into execution. This is a very different matter from holding that all discussion of the desirability of resorting to violence for political purposes should be ruthlessly stamped out. . . .

The United States is the last place on earth where mere talk about resistance and revolution ought to be treated as inherently vicious and intolerable. The founders of the colonies broke the religious laws of England before they came here and some of them engaged in large-sized rebellion. . . .

If a federal statute against the advocacy of force and violence had been enacted in the Abolition period, several distinguished citizens of Massachusetts would have been criminals. . . . we cannot draw a distinction between those days and ours on the ground that the government was bad then and is now good. I believe that to be true, but time alone will prove which is right. . . . We must not forget how Braxfield justified his ferocious sentences by saying that the British Constitution of 1794 was the best in the world. . . . the advocates of repression in those days were not a race of tyrants. They were respectable citizens like ourselves. They were merely mistaken. Can we be any more sure of our infallibility than of theirs? . . . There are many ways of fighting. The American policy is to meet force by force, and talk by talk. . . .

Until 1917 we stuck by the schoolboy maxim, "Sticks
and stones will break my bones, but words will never hurt
me". . . . . If there is any immediate danger of revolution,
the government should be employing the Criminal Code
instead of fooling around with a sedition law. . . . we
shall be wise if we seek remedial and not punitive methods
to make . . . talk of no effect. . . .

A Sedition Law is applied in ways which were wholly
unexpected when it was enacted. . . . it will be a very
difficult statute to construe unless the courts adhere closely
to the ordinary rules of criminal attempt. . . . Judges and
jurymen are trained to decide about overt acts, but problems of "subtle" propaganda are an entirely different matter. . . . the jury are cut loose entirely from overt acts and
the world of the five senses. They are adrift on a sea of
speculation.

At the very outset the same controversy will arise as in
Masses v. *Patten*. It is the old question of Mark Antony's
funeral oration. . . .

Let me illustrate this danger of loose interpretation from
the experience of the courts with an existing federal statute,
which looks absolutely clear-cut. This law . . . punishes
with imprisonment up to five years a willful "threat to take
the life of the President. . . ." What could be plainer?
. . . Let us see what kind of persons have been convicted
under this statute. A Syracuse woman of German descent,
exasperated by her fellow-employees who continually picked
on her and called her the Kaiser, finally burst out that
she would poison the President if she had him there.
She pleaded guilty . . . and was fined $300, "not because
the court regarded her as a dangerous person, but to show
all quick-tempered or alien-minded persons that they must
not threaten to do the President bodily harm or utter unpa-
triotic sentiments in such times as these." In another case,
the words were, "I wish Wilson was in hell, and if I had
the power I would put him there." The judges held this
revolting language to be a threat to kill the President, because how could he be in hell unless he were dead?

. . . men who use revolutionary language should not be
suppressed in the absence of very serious and pressing dan-

ger, because they almost always have a grievance. . . .
The agitator would be much wiser and more effective if he
expressed his case calmly without threats, but we ought not
to punish him for this mistake. He is not an educated
man. . . . he is not accustomed to weighing his words
carefully. . . . The worse the grievance, the more likely
the victim is to get angry and urge violent measures. Yet
that is the grievance which most needs removal. . . . Nor
will this treatment silence those who are really dangerous. . . . A passage in President Wilson's Message to
Congress in December, 1919, hammers this truth home:

> The only way to keep men from agitating against
> grievances is to remove the grievances. An unwilling-
> ness even to discuss these matters produces only dissat-
> isfaction and gives comfort to the extreme elements in
> our country which endeavor to stir up disturbances
> in order to provoke Governments to embark upon a
> course of retaliation and repression. The seed of revo-
> lution is repression.

. . . Nothing adds more to men's hatred for government than its refusal to let them talk, especially if they are
the type of person anarchists are, to whom talking a little
wildly is the greatest joy of life. Besides, suppression of
their mere words shows a fear of them, which only encour-
ages them to greater activity in secret. A widespread belief
is aroused that the government would not be so anxious to
silence its critics unless what they have been saying is true.
A wise and salutary neglect of talk, coupled with vigorous
measures against plans for actual violence and a general
endeavor to end discontent, is the best legal policy toward
anarchy and criminal syndicalism.

To quote from an extra-judicial decision of Justice
Holmes:

> With effervescing opinions, as with the not yet for-
> gotten champagnes, the quickest way to let them get
> flat is to let them get exposed to the air.

*On the other side of the argument are not only those
who would prohibit the advocacy of* violent overthrow of

government, but some who would even curb proposals to overthrow our form of government by democratic processes.

Ernest Van Den Haag:[17]

At present organized attempts to persuade citizens to bring antidemocratic groups to power by the ballot are lawful. Yet I believe that the pursuit of subversive aims even by peaceful means should be outlawed. . . . Even if Communists were peaceful, democrats could not peacefully accept defeat by them. Defeat at the polls is acceptable as long as the losers have the implicit assurance of the victors that the game will go on. They can try again; there is always another election. But if Communists were to win, the losers would not be allowed to play again. . . .

The fathers of our Constitution were successful in protecting us against a government that might keep itself in power by taking away our rights. Less attention was paid to the possibility that some citizens might *give away* their democratic birthright and invite others to do so, as large groups abroad have done. Yet if our right to choose the government freely is *inalienable*, then we are not entitled to *give* the right away any more than the government is entitled to take it away. . . . Nor, if freedom is to be inalienable, can invitations to alienate it be recognized as a legitimate part of the democratic process. . . .

But there is more: by installing a government which is to be the irremovable and total master of their fate, those voting to become *voluntary* political slaves would necessarily compel some of their fellows into *involuntary* servitude. They would not only irreversibly mortgage their own future; they would also deprive of political freedom those who want to keep it. . . . You may be entitled to suicide, but not to homicide. Yet unless the decision to abolish po-

---

[17] Reprinted by permission of the publisher and author from Ernest Van Den Haag, "Controlling Subversive Groups," *Annals of the American Academy of Political and Social Science* (July, 1955), pp. 62-71. For an elaboration of these views see also Ralph Ross and Ernest Van Den Haag, *The Fabric of Society* (New York: Harcourt, Brace & World, Inc., 1957), pp. 631-34, 645-55.

litical liberty is unanimous, the suicide necessarily would
become homicide. . . .

Nor is this all. . . . To allow citizens to vote against
democracy is to allow them to sell their children into slavery.

We are the beneficiaries of freedoms won in the past.
We possess but we do not own this precious heritage. We
have a right to use it but not to give it away or to destroy it.
We are trustees, not owners; and we cannot give away what
is not ours. . . .

It is earnestly feared that free speech would be destroyed
if invitations to destroy free speech—to surrender democracy—were disallowed. But could a law to preserve democratic freedom not be so drafted and interpreted that it
does not defeat its purpose? . . .

The meaning of "antidemocratic" is hardly open to
doubt. For instance, propaganda for socialism is not anti-
democratic as long as the changes are to be accomplished
through a free vote and as long as the Socialist government
does not propose to eliminate that freedom in the future.
Nor would propaganda to change the manner of voting or
restrict the franchise (for instance by increasing the voting
age to twenty-three or by denying the vote to women) be
antidemocratic. (An age or sex group is not a political
group. However, income or occupational groups could
probably not be disenfranchised without impairing democracy.)

*To the foregoing point of view two other authors offer
these rejoinders.*

Sidney Hook:[18]

Must a democracy make the democratic principle an un-
challengeable axiom in political thought? . . . Shall we, in
the name of democracy, refuse to permit democracy to be
judged for fear of losing it forever? Grant that the fear and

[18] Reprinted by permission of the publisher from Sidney Hook, *Paradoxes of Freedom* (Berkeley: University of California Press, 1962), pp.
135-37.

danger are there. Is the only way of meeting it the conversion of a democratic principle into an absolute presupposition? If it is, in what way does a democracy of this sort logically differ from a form of despotism—however enlightened or benevolent? We are told that "when necessary we must restrict the people's rule to conserve their liberty." Is this not equivalent to abandoning the majority principle and substituting the rule of the watchful minority who must set themselves up as the perpetual guardians of the liberties of their wards—the people? . . .

Is it permissible for a majority to alienate the freedom of a minority together with its own? No, not if one believes in freedom. But if the majority does not believe in freedom, even though as a minority we may fiercely complain and forcibly resist it, we cannot charge it with inconsistency. If the majority does believe in freedom, and prevents the minority which wishes to alienate its own and others' freedom from doing so, the minority in this instance has the same formal right to complaint and can take the same risk of action. There is no logical inconsistency here either. . . .

The same considerations hold in considering the argument that the surrender of a democracy by any majority is "undemocratic" because it binds future generations. No decision irrevocably binds future generations. The decision to uphold a democratic system does not obligate future generations to preserve it; the decision to surrender it does not prevent future generations from restoring it.

Any political system which accepts the premise that a people must be forced to be free seems to me to be psychologically defective. Freedom—like loyalty, like love—by the very nature of the human emotions involved, cannot be commanded.

Alan Barth:[19]

. . . paradoxically, loyalty in a free society depends upon the toleration of disloyalty. The loyalty of free men

---

[19] Reprinted by permission of the publisher and author from Alan Barth, *The Loyalty of Free Men* (New York: The Viking Press, 1951), p. 231.

must be freely given—which is to say, that those who give it must be genuinely free to withhold it. Nothing is more fundamental to freedom than that this choice be a real one.

Some may regard it as the height of academic theorizing to worry what to do in the unlikelihood of a campaign for public office in which one contestant openly states that, upon being elected, he will abolish future elections. But the question does force us back to a serious examination of our basic political philosophy. To accept the Van Den Haag position, which would not even chance the outcome of our hypothetical election, is really to abandon faith in the democratic process in favor of "democracy by fiat"— surely a contradiction in terms. But to follow Hook's alternative is not only to tolerate the advocacy of abandoning democracy but also to accept an act of abandonment by the implementation of an anti-democratic majority vote. Thus Hook, while rejecting absolutism as a mode of adherence to democratic beliefs, is willing absolutely to submit to any kind of rule a majority may in fact choose to impose—also surely a contradiction.

Perhaps the dilemma is irresolvable. But, in closing this chapter, we would offer for discussion another possibility. (We do this in the spirit of devil's advocacy, for the position to be set forth is not one to which the author is completely committed, but merely one he feels worthy of serious consideration.) If the advocates of overthrow propose violent revolution, we would let them talk but not act. If they propose peaceful change, we would let them speak, and we would let the majority elect them if they wished. But if, after the election, it appeared clear that upon assuming office they would indeed establish a dictatorship, we would at that point use whatever power of government we could still muster to try to stop them. We would not attempt to justify such action with democratic principles. We would simply take the position that if matters are to be settled henceforth by power rather than by discussion and vote, we would rather have ourselves in the saddle than them. Why hand them our gun only to try, unarmed, to take it back?

QUESTIONS FOR DISCUSSION

1. Is there any formula by which a speech such as Mark Antony's funeral oration could be punished without interfering, under the same rule, with much talk that is quite harmless?

2. It is sometimes claimed that Justice Holmes had little justifiable cause for complaint about the outcome of the Abrams and Gitlow cases, having ruled as he did in the earlier cases of Schenck, Frohwerk, and Debs. To what extent, if any, is this a fair evaluation of Holmes' positions?

3. If, as Justice Holmes asserts in his Gitlow dissent, "every idea is an incitement," can any sensible distinctions be maintained between permissible and forbidden speech in the area of the advocacy of political change?

4. West Virginia State Board of Education v. Barnette is often classified as a "freedom of religion" rather than a "freedom of speech" case. What rationale can be offered for the latter classification?

5. Do the dissenting opinions in Dennis and Scales have anything in common with the much earlier case of De Jonge?

6. What are the implications of the statement in Dennis rejecting "the contention that success or probability of success" is a valid criterion for measuring whether advocacy of overthrow of government may be suppressed? Is the Court's position here an acceptable one?

7. The distinction drawn in Yates between urging listeners to believe something and urging them to do something is one that is frequently made in speech textbooks. Is it a valid distinction?

8. What, if anything, does The New York Times have in common with Near? How does it differ?

9. What strengths and weaknesses are there in the arguments offered by Van Den Haag, Hook, and the author of

this book regarding the advocacy of the abolition of democracy?

10. How satisfactory is Van Den Haag's definition of "anti-democratic" propaganda?

3

Artistic Expression
and the
Problem of Public Morality

"My opinion is that there would never have been
an infidel, if there had never been a priest."
—Thomas Jefferson,
Letter to Mrs. Harrison Smith

TWO MASSACHUSETTS STORIES
AND ONE ACROSS THE NATION

From *The New York Times*

ROCKPORT, MASS., July 13, 1962—The Board of Selectmen here has banned two stage plays because they are
"quite sexy."

The board revealed last night that the plays, *Call Me by
My Rightful Name* and *The Zoo Story* cannot be produced
here as part of a five-play program from July 23 to September 2.

Ernest R. Poole, Jr., chairman of the Board of Selectmen,
announced the decision.

"We approved three plays," he said, "but the other two
were read and they were quite sexy. We would not grant
permission for those two because we did not think they
should be shown in Rockport because they were off-
color." . . .

Both *Call Me by My Rightful Name* and *The Zoo Story*
are first efforts by Michael Shurtleff and Edward Albee,

respectively. Both plays were done Off Broadway and brought acclaim to the authors.

BOSTON, September 3, 1963—Richard J. Sinnott, the city censor, has requested the road company of Edward Albee's play, *Who's Afraid of Virginia Woolf?* to eliminate "irreverent" references to the Deity and to reduce profanity in future performances here. . . .

Jack Toohey, press agent for the touring company, said that the changes "were made on a request basis and we will comply."

NEW YORK, April 5, 1964—Lenny Bruce pleaded not guilty yesterday to a charge of giving an indecent performance in a Greenwich Village coffeehouse. Judge Vincent P. Rao in Criminal Court released the comedian in $1,000 bail. . . .

Mr. Bruce, who is 38, was arrested Friday night at the café. Plainclothes men attended a performance at the club last Sunday and made a recording of the act. Mr. Bruce has been arrested twice before, in Los Angeles, on charges of obscenity in his night club act. [He has also been arrested in Chicago and San Francisco on the same charge.]

Probably no free speech controversies in the United States stimulate the flow of as much public adrenalin as those surrounding the communication of allegedly immoral words and scenes. Battle lines have been drawn in local communities and in the courts between many conflicting interest groups—self-appointed vigilantes of community morals, official censoring bodies, publishers, librarians, pornography profiteers, avant-garde artists and other producers of daring communication, clergymen, and philosophical libertarians—all with strong emotional commitments in the fray. The issues are similar whether the work in question be a book, a magazine, a movie, a play, a radio or TV program, or a night club act, and may be phrased as follows:

1. *May a majority, acting in the alleged interest of public morality, prohibit the expression or portrayal of*

ideas and feelings which it regards as immoral or in bad taste?

2. Should different treatment be accorded to communication depending upon whether it stimulates "normal" sexual desires, appeals to "abnormal" sexual interests, is scatological (dealing in images related to excrement), profane (dealing irreverently with religious concepts), or portrays violence? Is there a basis for assuming that any or all of these is conducive to anti-social or illegal behavior?

3. Can a valid distinction be made between pure entertainment and the communication of ideas? Are there certain kinds of communication which have no social importance or value whatsoever?

4. Is it possible, and desirable, to establish different standards for the permissibility of communication depending upon whether the audience consists of children or adults?

5. Are different standards justified on the basis of whether communication is written or oral, or on the basis of whether oral communication occurs via radio, TV, motion pictures, theater, or night club?

6. At what point, if any, do extra-legal pressures against disliked communication become sufficiently coercive to run afoul of the protections of the constitution?

———————◆———————

As in the case of political heresy, legal conflict over allegedly immoral artistic expression has been largely a phenomenon of the twentieth century, and more particularly of the era since World War I. If problems existed before this, and there are instances we know about, they tended to be dealt with by informal community action. With the coming of mass media of communication, however, the controversies have grown to national scope and have tended to be brought for settlement into our courts of law. The first major case involving movie censorship to reach the U. S. Supreme Court was in 1915 (Mutual Film Corporation v. Ohio Industrial Commission, 236 US 230), when the Court suggested that since motion pictures were a form of commercial entertainment, they were not protected from censorship by the free speech clause of the First Amendment. But by 1948, in a case involving an antitrust action against the block-booking of movies rather than a case of censorship of movie content, Justice Douglas' opinion for the Court included a dictum which foreshadowed the rejection of the Mutual Film doctrine (United States v. Paramount Pictures, 334 US 133). The explicit reversal, as we shall see, was to occur four years later in Burstyn v. Wilson, which brought motion pictures back within the ambit of the Bill of Rights and gave rise to a string of cases which ensued during the following decade.

Meanwhile, in the realm of written communication, the clash between libertarian and censor was catching fire. In 1930, Congress amended a tariff act that had formerly authorized customs officials to bar entry into the country of "objectionable" literature. The new law made an exception for classics and works of recognized literary merit, and also required the government to obtain a court order to authorize confiscation of a book. When, in 1933, customs officials attempted to obtain such an order to confiscate James Joyce's Ulysses, their motion was denied by Federal District Judge Woolsey, whose decision was affirmed by the Court of Appeals (United States v. One Book Called "Ulysses," 5 F Supp 182 and 72 F 2d 705). Said Judge Woolsey:

> . . . in *Ulysses*, in spite of its unusual frankness, I do not detect anywhere the leer of the sensualist. I hold, therefore, that it is not pornographic.

In 1946, the U. S. Supreme Court was confronted with another act of censorship by the executive branch of government, this time in the form of a denial by the Postmaster General of second-class mailing privileges to Esquire magazine on the grounds that some of its articles and pictures were "morally improper and not for the public welfare. . . ." A unanimous Court, speaking through Justice Douglas, sustained an injunction against the Postmaster General's order and stated that "a requirement that literature or art conform to some norm prescribed by an official smacks of an ideology foreign to our system" (Hannegan v. Esquire, Inc., 327 US 146).

Two years later the Supreme Court dealt with two other important cases. In the first, the Court reversed the conviction of a New York City bookdealer who had been charged with violation of a state obscenity law. The Court held that the statute's definition of the offense was too vague to stand (Winters v. New York, 333 US 507). But in the second case, involving a New York ban on Edmund Wilson's Memoirs of Hecate County, the justices could not agree. Justice Frankfurter had abstained from the case because of personal friendship with the author, leaving only eight voting justices, who split 4-4. Thus the decision of the lower court was left standing (Doubleday & Company v. New York, 355 US 848). To this day, paperback copies of Memoirs of Hecate County sold throughout the United States bear these statements on the cover:

One of the Twentieth Century's Outstanding Books by America's Foremost Living Critic

Not for Sale in New York State

The division over this book may be viewed as somewhat symptomatic of the ambivalence regarding the problem of obscenity which has characterized the Supreme Court and the American public in the years that have followed.

One of the most libertarian judicial statements written on the obscenity issue came a year after the Memoirs of Hecate County case, from a lower court in Pennsylvania. A bookseller had been indicted under the penal code for possessing, with intent to sell, nine novels, four of them by James Farrell and two by William Faulkner. In adjudicating this case, Judge Bok, whose decision was sustained by the Pennsylvania Supreme Court, insisted that obscenity convictions be limited to "dirt for dirt's sake," and then only when a causal connection to illegal behavior could be demonstrated.

COMMONWEALTH v. GORDON [1]

JUDGE BOK:

. . . The full weight of the legislative prohibition dangles from the word "obscene" and its synonyms. Nowhere are these words defined; nowhere is the danger to be expected of them stated; nowhere is a standard of judgment set forth. I assume that "obscenity" is expected to have a familiar and inherent meaning, both as to what it is and as to what it does.

It is my purpose to show that it has no such inherent meaning; that different meanings given to it at different times are not constant, either historically or legally; and that it is not constitutionally indictable unless it takes the form of sexual impurity, i.e., "dirt for dirt's sake" and can be traced to actual criminal behavior, either actual or demonstrably imminent.

. . . Far from inciting to lewd or lecherous desires, which are sensorially pleasurable, these books leave one either with a sense of horror or a pity for the degradation of mankind. The effect upon the normal reader . . . would be anything but what the vice hunters fear it might be. . . .

It will be asked whether one would care to have one's young daughter read these books. I suppose that by the time she is old enough to wish to read them she will have learned the biologic facts of life and the words that go with them. There is something seriously wrong at home if those facts have not been met and faced and sorted by then; it is not children so much as parents that should receive our concern about this. I should prefer that my own three daughters meet the facts of life and the literature of the world in my library than behind a neighbor's barn, for I can face the adversary there directly. If the young ladies are appalled by what they read, they can close the book at the bottom of page one; if they read further, they will learn what is in the world and in its people, and no parents who

have been discerning with their children need fear the outcome. Nor can they hold it back, for life is a series of little
battles and minor issues, and the burden of choice is on us
all, every day, young and old. Our daughters must live in
the world and decide what sort of women they are to be,
and we should be willing to prefer their deliberate and informed choice of decency rather than an innocence that
continues to spring from ignorance. If that choice be made
in the open sunlight, it is more apt than when made in
shadow to fall on the side of honorable behavior. . . .

Censorship, which is the policeman of decency, whether
religious, patriotic, or moral, has had distinct fashions, depending on which great questions were agitating society at
the time. During the Middle Ages, when the church was
supreme, the focus of suppression was upon heresy and
blasphemy. When the State became uppermost, the focus
of suppression was upon treason and sedition. The advent
of technology made Queen Victoria realize, perhaps sub-
consciously, that loose morals would theaten the peace of
mind necessary to the development of invention and big
business; the focus moved to sexual morality. . . .

Something might be said . . . about the familiar four-
letter words that are so often associated with sexual impurity.
These are, almost without exception, of honest Anglo-
Saxon ancestry, and were not invented for purely scatological effect. The one, for example, that is used to denote the
sexual act is an old agricultural word meaning "to plant,"
and was at one time a wholly respectable member of the
English vocabulary. The distinction between a word of
decent etymological history and one of smut alone is important; it shows that fashions in language change as expect-
ably as do the concepts of what language connotes. It is
the old business of semantics again, the difference between
word and concept. . . .

Censorship should be the proper activity of the community rather than of the law, and the community has never
been lazy upholding what it believes to be inherently decent at the moment. . . . the market place is the best cru-
cible in which to distil an instinctive morality. . . . This is

healthy, for it is the struggle of free opinion; it is not suppression by law. . . .

———————

The U. S. Supreme Court, as we shall find, was to comment on Judge Bok's opinion several years later. In the meanwhile the problem of motion picture censorship took center stage. In 1952, as indicated earlier, the Court decided to grant to movies the protections of the free speech clause of the constitution. The occasion was the refusal by the state of New York to grant a license for the showing of an Italian film, The Miracle, which depicted the story of a simple-minded girl who imagines herself the instrument of a virgin birth. A long and bitter conflict involving the New York City Commissioner of Licenses, the Paris Theatre, Francis Cardinal Spellman, and many others, preceded the final determination by the State Board of Regents that the picture was "sacrilegious." The Supreme Court, though yet unwilling to tackle the constitutionality of motion picture licensing per se, was fully prepared to reject sacrilegiousness as a valid basis for state interference.

BURSTYN, INC. v. WILSON [2]

MR. JUSTICE CLARK delivered the opinion of the Court. . . . In a series of decisions beginning with *Gitlow* v. *People of State of New York*, . . . this Court held that the liberty of speech and of the press which the First Amendment guarantees against abridgment by the federal government is within the liberty safeguarded by the Due Process Clause of the Fourteenth Amendment from invasion by state action. That principle has been followed and reaffirmed to the present day. Since this series of decisions came after the *Mutual* decision, the present case is the first to present squarely to us the question whether motion pictures are within the ambit of protection which the First Amendment, through the Fourteenth, secures to any form of "speech" or "the press."

———————

[2] 343 US 495 (1952).

It cannot be doubted that motion pictures are a significant medium for the communication of ideas. They may affect public attitudes and behavior in a variety of ways, ranging from direct espousal of a political or social doctrine to the subtle shaping of thought which characterizes all artistic expression. The importance of motion pictures as an organ of public opinion is not lessened by the fact that they are designed to entertain as well as to inform. . . .

It is urged that motion pictures do not fall within the First Amendment's aegis because their production, distribution, and exhibition is a large-scale business conducted for private profit. We cannot agree. That books, newspapers, and magazines are published and sold for profit does not prevent them from being a form of expression whose liberty is safeguarded by the First Amendment. We fail to see why operation for profit should have any different effect in the case of motion pictures.

It is further urged that motion pictures possess a greater capacity for evil, particularly among the youth of a community, than other modes of expression. Even if one were to accept this hypothesis, it does not follow that motion pictures should be disqualified from First Amendment protection. If there be capacity for evil it may be relevant in determining the permissible scope of community control, but it does not authorize substantially unbridled censorship such as we have here.

For the foregoing reasons, we conclude that expression by means of motion pictures is included within the free speech and free press guaranty of the First and Fourteenth Amendments. To the extent that language in the opinion in *Mutual Film Corp.* v. *Industrial Comm.*, *supra*, is out of harmony with the views here set forth, we no longer adhere to it.

. . . It does not follow that the Constitution requires absolute freedom to exhibit every motion picture of every kind at all times and all places. . . . Nor does it follow that motion pictures are necessarily subject to the precise rules governing any other particular method of expression. Each method tends to present its own peculiar problems.

But the basic principles of freedom of speech and the press, like the First Amendment's command, do not vary.

New York's highest court says there is "nothing mysterious" about the statutory provision applied in this case: "It is simply this: that no religion, as that word is understood by the ordinary, reasonable person, shall be treated with contempt, mockery, scorn and ridicule. . . ." This is far from the kind of narrow exception to freedom of expression which a state may carve out to satisfy the adverse demands of other interests of society. In seeking to apply the broad and all-inclusive definition of "sacrilegious" given by the New York courts, the censor is set adrift upon a boundless sea amid a myriad of conflicting currents of religious views, with no charts but those provided by the most vocal and powerful orthodoxies. . . . Application of the "sacrilegious" test, in these or other respects, might raise substantial questions under the First Amendment's guaranty of separate church and state with freedom of worship for all. However, from the standpoint of freedom of speech and the press, it is enough to point out that the state has no legitimate interest in protecting any or all religions from views distasteful to them which is sufficient to justify prior restraints upon the expression of those views. . . .

Since the term "sacrilegious" is the sole standard under attack here, it is not necessary for us to decide, for example, whether a state may censor motion pictures under a clearly-drawn statute designed and applied to prevent the showing of obscene films. That is a very different question from the one now before us. We hold only that under the First and Fourteenth Amendments a state may not ban a film on the basis of a censor's conclusion that it is "sacrilegious."

Reversed.

Close on the heels of the Burstyn *decision, and employing the same rationale, the U. S. Supreme Court struck down three other acts of motion picture censorship. The movies in question were* Pinky, *the story of an interracial romance, which had been banned in Marshall, Texas, as "prejudicial to the best interests of the city"* (Gelling v.

Texas, 343 US 960); La Ronde, a French film, barred from New York as "immoral;" and M, a murder story, refused a license in Ohio because it "depicted scenes of crime." All of these criteria were rejected as impermissible bases for censorship. But in the latter two cases, combined in one decision, Justices Douglas and Black would have gone even farther, to invalidate all prior censorship of films.

SUPERIOR FILMS v. DEPARTMENT OF EDUCATION COMMERCIAL PICTURES v. REGENTS OF THE STATE OF NEW YORK [3]

MR. JUSTICE DOUGLAS, with whom MR. JUSTICE BLACK agrees, concurring.

The argument of Ohio and New York that the government may establish censorship over moving pictures is one I cannot accept. . . . Certainly a system, still in force in some nations, which required a newspaper to submit to a board its news items, editorials, and cartoons before it published them could not be sustained. Nor could book publishers be required to submit their novels, poems, and tracts to censors for clearance before publication. . . .

Nor is it conceivable to me that producers of plays for the legitimate theatre or for television could be required to submit their manuscripts to censors on pain of penalty for producing them without approval. Certainly the spoken word is as freely protected against prior restraints as that which is written. Such indeed is the force of our decision in *Thomas* v. *Collins*. . . . The freedom of the platform which it espouses carries with it freedom of the stage.

The same result in the case of motion pictures necessarily follows as a consequence of our holding in *Joseph Burstyn* v. *Wilson* . . . that motion pictures are "within the free speech and free press guaranty of the First and Fourteenth Amendments."

Motion pictures are of course a different medium of expression than the public speech, the radio, the stage, the novel, or the magazine. But the First Amendment draws no distinction between the various methods of communicating

---

[3] 346 US 587 (1953).

ideas. On occasion one may be more powerful or effective than another. The movie, like the public speech, radio, or television, is transitory—here now and gone in an instant. The novel, the short story, the poem in printed form are permanently at hand to reenact the drama or to retell the story over and again. Which medium will give the most excitement and have the most enduring effect will vary with the theme and the actors. It is not for the censor to determine in any case. The First and Fourteenth Amendments say that Congress and the States shall make "no law" which abridges freedom of speech or of the press. In order to sanction a system of censorship I would have to say that "no law" does not mean what it says, that "no law" is qualified to mean "some" laws. I cannot take that step.

In this Nation every writer, actor, or producer, no matter what medium of expression he may use, should be freed from the censor.

Five years later, turning again to books, the Supreme Court reaffirmed the unwillingness to abandon all methods of prior restraint that it had shown with respect to movies, and upheld a New York injunction issued under what the majority regarded as acceptable procedures.

KINGSLEY BOOKS, INC. v. BROWN [4]

Mr. Justice Frankfurter delivered the opinion of the Court.

This is a proceeding under . . . the New York Code of Criminal Procedure . . . authorizing the chief executive, or legal officer, of a municipality to invoke a "limited injunctive remedy," under closely defined procedural safeguards, against the sale and distribution of written and printed matter found after due trial to be obscene. . . . the judge . . . found that the booklets annexed to the complaint . . . were clearly obscene—were "dirt for dirt's sake"; he enjoined their further distribution and ordered their destruction. He refused to enjoin "the sale and distri-

---

[4] 354 US 436 (1957).

bution of later issues" on the ground that "to rule against a volume not offered in evidence would . . . impose an unreasonable prior restraint". . . . Just as *Near* v. *Minnesota* . . . left no doubts that "Liberty of speech, and of the press, is also not an absolute right," . . . it likewise made clear that "the protection even as to previous restraint is not absolutely unlimited." . . . To be sure, the limitation is the exception; it is to be closely confined so as to preclude what may fairly be deemed licensing or censorship. . . . The phrase "prior restraint" is not a self-wielding sword. Nor can it serve as a talismanic test. The duty of closer analysis and critical judgment in applying the thought behind the phrase has thus been authoritatively put by one who brings weighty learning to his support of constitutionally protected liberties: "What is needed," writes Professor Paul Freund, "is a pragmatic assessment of its operation in particular circumstances. The generalization that prior restraint is particularly obnoxious in civil liberties cases must yield to more particularistic analysis." . . .

Mr. Chief Justice Warren, dissenting.

. . . It is the manner of use that should determine obscenity. It is the conduct of the individual that should be judged, not the quality of art or literature. . . . in the absence of a prior judicial determination of illegal use, books, pictures and other objects of expression should not be destroyed. It savors too much of book burning.

I would reverse.

———◆———

The problem of post facto punishment of obscenity also came before the high court in the same term, as the result of an arrest in New York of one Roth, a seller of books, photographs, and magazines, who was charged with mailing obscene circulars and advertising. When his conviction had reached the U. S. Second Circuit Court of Appeals, Judge Jerome Frank, though feeling obliged by legal precedent to concur in the conviction, was moved to write a provocative treatise which, in essence, asked the U. S. Supreme Court to liberate speech and press entirely from laws against obscenity.

UNITED STATES v. ROTH [5]

JUDGE FRANK, concurring.

. . . I agree with my colleagues that, since ours is an inferior court, we should not hold invalid a statute which our superior has thus often said is constitutional. . . . Yet I think it not improper to set forth . . . considerations concerning the obscenity statute's validity with which, up to now, I think the Supreme Court has not dealt in any of its opinions. . . . I happen not to be interested in so-called "pornography"; and I think defendant's motives obnoxious. But if the statute were invalid, the merit of those publications would be irrelevant. . . . So, too, as to defendant's motives. . . . those who in the 20th Century endorse legislation suppressing "obscene" literature have an attitude towards freedom of expression which does not match that of the framers of the First Amendment . . . but does stem from an attitude, towards writings dealing with sex, which arose decades later, in the mid-19th Century, and is therefore labelled—doubtless too sweepingly— "Victorian." It was a dogma of "Victorian morality" that sexual misbehavior would be encouraged if one were to "acknowledge its existence or at any rate to present it vividly enough to form a life-like image of it in the reader's mind"; this morality rested on a "faith that you could best conquer evil by shutting your eyes to its existence." . . . The demands at that time for "decency" in published words did not comport with the actual sexual conduct of many of those who made those demands. . . .

As I have said, I have no doubt the jury could reasonably find, beyond a reasonable doubt, that many of the publications mailed by defendant were obscene within the current judicial definition. . . . But so, too, are a multitude of recognized works of art found in public libraries. . . .

To the argument that such books (and such reproduc-

---

[5] 237 F. 2d 796 (2d Cir. 1956).

tions of famous paintings and works of sculpture) fall within the statutory ban, the courts have answered that they are "classics." . . . There is a "curious dilemma" involved in this answer that the statute condemns "only books which are dull and without merit," . . . No one can reconcile the currently accepted test of obscenity with the immunity of such "classics" as e.g. Aristophanes' Lysistrata, Chaucer's Canterbury Tales, Rabelais' Gargantua and Pantagruel, Shakespeare's Venus and Adonis, Fielding's Tom Jones. . . . For such "obscene" writings, just because of their greater artistry and charm, will presumably have far greater influence on readers than dull inartistic writings.

It will not do to differentiate a "classic," published in the past, on the ground that it comported with the average moral attitudes at the time and place of its original publication. Often this was not true. It was not true, for instance, of Balzac's Droll Stories. . . .

The truth is that the courts have exempted the "classics" from the federal obscenity statute, since otherwise most Americans would be deprived of access to many masterpieces of literature and the pictorial arts, and a statute yielding such deprivation would not only be laughably absurd but would squarely oppose the intention of the cultivated men who framed and adopted the First Amendment.

This exception—nowhere to be found in the statute—is a judge-made device invented to avoid that absurdity. The fact that the judges have felt the necessity of seeking that avoidance, serves to suggest forcibly that the statute, in its attempt to control what our citizens may read and see, violates the First Amendment. For no one can rationally justify the judge-made exception. . . .

. . . Originality, not too plentiful, should be cherished, not stifled. An author's imagination may be cramped if he must write with one eye on prosecutors or juries; authors must cope with publishers who, fearful about the judgments of governmental censors, may refuse to accept the manuscripts of contemporary Shelleys or Mark Twains or Whitmans. . . .

When the Roth case reached the Supreme Court, the justices, except for Black and Douglas, were not ready to follow the robust libertarianism of Judge Frank or even the more moderate liberality of Judge Bok, both of whose views the majority opinion explicitly rejected. Instead, Justice Brennan declared that obscenity, as he proceeded to define it for the Court, is not permissible speech. It is interesting to note that under the Roth definition of obscenity, the ultimate test of a communication's permissibility is the reaction of the audience—"the average person, applying contemporary community standards"—just as in the "fighting words" doctrine of the Chaplinsky case the test was what "men of common intelligence" would regard as likely to cause a fight.

ROTH v. UNITED STATES
ALBERTS v. CALIFORNIA [6]

MR. JUSTICE BRENNAN delivered the opinion of the Court.

. . . The dispositive question is whether obscenity is utterance within the area of protected speech and press. Although this is the first time the question has been squarely presented to this Court, either under the First Amendment or under the Fourteenth Amendment, expressions found in numerous opinions indicate that this Court has always assumed that obscenity is not protected by the freedoms of speech and press. . . .

The guaranties of freedom of expression in effect in 10 of the 14 States which by 1792 had ratified the Constitution, gave no absolute protection for every utterance. Thirteen of the 14 States provided for the prosecution of libel, and all of those States made either blasphemy or profanity, or both, statutory crimes. As early as 1712, Massachusetts made it criminal to publish "any filthy, obscene, or profane song, pamphlet, libel or mock sermon" in imitation or mimicking of religious services. . . . Thus, profanity and obscenity were related offenses.

---

[6] 354 US 476 (1957).

In light of this history, it is apparent that the unconditional phrasing of the First Amendment was not intended to protect every utterance. This phrasing did not prevent this Court from concluding that libelous utterances are not within the area of constitutionally protected speech. *Beauharnais* v. *Illinois* . . . At the time of the adoption of the First Amendment, obscenity law was not as fully developed as libel law, but there is sufficiently contemporaneous evidence to show that obscenity, too, was outside the protection intended for speech and press.

The protection given speech and press was fashioned to assure unfettered interchange of ideas for the bringing about of political and social changes desired by the people. . . .

All ideas having even the slightest redeeming social importance—unorthodox ideas, controversial ideas, even ideas hateful to the prevailing climate of opinion—have the full protection of the guaranties, unless excludable because they encroach upon the limited area of more important interests. But implicit in the history of the First Amendment is the rejection of obscenity as utterly without redeeming social importance. This rejection for that reason is mirrored in the universal judgment that obscenity should be restrained, reflected in the international agreement of over 50 nations, in the obscenity laws of all of the 48 States, and in the 20 obscenity laws enacted by the Congress from 1842 to 1956. . . .

We hold that obscenity is not within the area of constitutionally protected speech or press. . . .

However, sex and obscenity are not synonymous. Obscene material is material which deals with sex in a manner appealing to prurient interest. . . .

The early leading standard of obscenity allowed material to be judged merely by the effect of an isolated excerpt upon particularly susceptible persons [*Regina* v. *Hicklin*]. . . . Some American courts adopted this standard but later decisions have rejected it and substituted this test: whether to the average person, applying contemporary community standards, the dominant theme of the material taken as a whole appeals to prurient interest. . . .

Mr. Justice Douglas, with whom Mr. Justice Black concurs, dissenting.

When we sustain these convictions, we make the legality of a publication turn on the purity of thought which a book or tract instills in the mind of the reader. I do not think we can approve that standard and be faithful to the command of the First Amendment, which by its terms is a restraint on Congress and which by the Fourteenth is a restraint on the States.

. . . punishment is inflicted for thoughts provoked, not for overt acts nor antisocial conduct. This test cannot be squared with our decisions under the First Amendment. Even the ill-starred Dennis case conceded that speech to be punishable must have some relation to action which could be penalized by government. . . . This issue cannot be avoided by saying that obscenity is not protected by the First Amendment. The question remains, what is the constitutional test of obscenity?

The tests by which these convictions were obtained require only the arousing of sexual thoughts. Yet the arousing of sexual thoughts and desires happens every day in normal life in dozens of ways. . . .

The test of obscenity the Court endorses today gives the censor free range over a vast domain. . . .

If we were certain that impurity of sexual thoughts impelled to action, we would be on less dangerous ground in punishing the distributors of this sex literature. But it is by no means clear that obscene literature, as so defined, is a significant factor in influencing substantial deviations from the community standards. . . .

The absence of dependable information on the effect of obscene literature on human conduct should make us wary. It should put us on the side of protecting society's interest in literature, except and unless it can be said that the particular publication has an impact on action that the government can control. . . .

The standard of what offends "the common conscience of the community" conflicts, in my judgment, with the command of the First Amendment that "Congress shall make no law . . . abridging the freedom of speech, or of

the press." Certainly that standard would not be an acceptable one if religion, economics, politics or philosophy were
involved. How does it become a constitutional standard
when literature treating with sex is concerned?

Any test that turns on what is offensive to the community's standards is too loose, too capricious, too destructive
of freedom of expression to be squared with the First
Amendment. Under that test, juries can censor, suppress,
and punish what they don't like, provided the matter relates to "sexual impurity" or has a tendency "to excite lustful thoughts." This is community censorship in one of its
worst forms. It creates a regime where in the battle between the literati and the Philistines, the Philistines are
certain to win. If experience in this field teaches anything,
it is that "censorship of obscenity has almost always been
both irrational and indiscriminate." . . . The test adopted
here accentuates that trend.

. . . if the First Amendment guarantee of freedom of
speech and press is to mean anything in this field, it must
allow protests even against the moral code that the standard of the day sets for the community. In other words,
literature should not be suppressed merely because it
offends the moral code of the censor. . . .

I do not think that the problem can be resolved by the
Court's statement that "obscenity is not expression protected by the First Amendment." With the exception of
Beauharnais v. *Illinois*. . . . none of our cases has resolved
problems of free speech and free press by placing any form
of expression beyond the pale of the absolute prohibition of
the First Amendment. Unlike the law of libel, wrongfully
relied on in Beauharnais, there is no special historical evidence that literature dealing with sex was intended to be
treated in a special manner by those who drafted the First
Amendment. In fact, the first reported court decision in
this country involving obscene literature was in 1821. . . .
I reject too the implication that problems of freedom of
speech and of the press are to be resolved by weighing
against the values of free expression, the judgment of the
Court that a particular form of that expression has "no
redeeming social importance." The First Amendment, its

prohibition in terms absolute, was designed to preclude courts as well as legislatures from weighing the values of speech against silence. The First Amendment puts free speech in the preferred position.

Freedom of expression can be suppressed if, and to the extent that, it is so closely brigaded with illegal action as to be an inseparable part of it. *Giboney* v. *Empire Storage Co.* . . . As a people, we cannot afford to relax that standard. For the test that suppresses a cheap tract today can suppress a literary gem tomorrow. All it need do is to incite a lascivious thought or arouse a lustful desire. The list of books that judges or juries can place in that category is endless.

I would give the broad sweep of the First Amendment full support. I have the same confidence in the ability of our people to reject noxious literature as I have in their capacity to sort out the true from the false in theology, economics, politics, or any other field.

The Roth decision appeared at first to be an open invitation to censorial minded officials across the country to embark on a vast campaign of suppression. But the Supreme Court, during the same year, made it clear that no such blank check had been written. Just prior to Roth, with Justice Frankfurter writing their unanimous opinion, the justices had flatly declared unconstitutional a Michigan statute making it unlawful to disseminate any communication "tending to incite minors to violent or depraved or immoral acts, manifestly tending to the corruption of the morals of youth."

BUTLER v. MICHIGAN [7]

MR. JUSTICE FRANKFURTER delivered the opinion of the Court.

. . . The State insists that, by thus quarantining the general reading public against books not too rugged for grown men and women in order to shield juvenile innocence, it is exercising its power to promote the general welfare. Surely, this is to burn the house to roast the pig. . . .

---

[7] 352 US 380 (1957).

We have before us legislation not reasonably restricted to the evil with which it is said to deal. The incidence of this enactment is to reduce the adult population of Michigan to reading only what is fit for children.

During the same term, citing Roth as precedent, the Court struck down a Chicago ban on the movie The Game of Love, reminding the censors that sex per se is not obscene (Times Film Corporation v. City of Chicago, 355 US 35). The next year, again relying on the Roth definition of obscenity, the justices invalidated government interferences with the distribution of a homosexual magazine (One, Inc. v. Oleson, 355 US 371), and a nudist magazine (Sunshine Book Co. v. Summerfield, 355 US 372). In the latter case, their decision overruled what must surely be one of the most amazing court opinions ever written, in which the District Judge, reviewing the magazine in question page by page and photograph by photograph, discussed in laborious detail how prominent or how shadowed the human genitalia may be allowed to appear (Sunshine Book Co. v. Summerfield, 128 F Supp 565).

Still two years later, the Supreme Court further qualified the Roth decision. They found, in connection with the obscenity indictment of a California bookseller, that the conviction could not stand without proof of "scienter"—that is, that the bookseller knew the contents of the allegedly obscene volume he was selling (Smith v. California, 361 US 147). And, in the case of the movie version of Lady Chatterley's Lover, the approving portrayal of adultery was held to be an idea within the protection of the First Amendment.

KINGSLEY INTERNATIONAL PICTURES CORP. v. REGENTS OF UNIVERSITY OF STATE OF NEW YORK [8]

MR. JUSTICE STEWART delivered the opinion of the Court.

. . . A majority of the Court of Appeals ascribed . . .

---

[8] 360 US 684 (1959).

a precise purpose of the New York Legislature to require the denial of a license to a motion picture "because its subject matter is adultery presented as being right and desirable for certain people under certain circumstances."

We accept the premise that the motion picture here in question can be so characterized. We accept too, as we must, the construction of the New York Legislature's language which the Court of Appeals has put upon it. . . . That construction, we emphasize, gives to the term "sexual immorality" a concept entirely different from the concept embraced in words like "obscenity" or "pornography." Moreover, it is not suggested that the film would itself operate as an incitement to illegal action. Rather, the New York Court of Appeals tells us that the relevant portion of the New York Education Law requires the denial of a license to any motion picture which approvingly portrays an adulterous relationship, quite without reference to the manner of its portrayal.

What New York has done, therefore, is to prevent the exhibition of a motion picture because that picture advocates an idea—that adultery under certain circumstances may be proper behavior. Yet the First Amendment's basic guarantee is of freedom to advocate ideas. The State, quite simply, has thus struck at the very heart of constitutionally protected liberty.

It is contended that the State's action was justified because the motion picture attractively portrays a relationship which is contrary to the moral standards, the religious precepts, and the legal code of its citizenry. This argument misconceives what it is that the Constitution protects. Its guarantee is not confined to the expression of ideas that are conventional or shared by a majority. It protects advocacy of the opinion that adultery may sometimes be proper, no less than advocacy of socialism or the single tax. And in the realm of ideas it protects expression which is eloquent no less than that which is unconvincing.

———————◆———————

Encouraged by the Court's seeming movement toward increasing liberality, Times Film Corporation decided the time had come to force a head-on decision on the question of the licensing of movies per se. The majority of the justices, as we have seen, had managed thus far to avoid that broad issue by striking down, in each specific case that arose, the particular criterion used for suppression. This test was accomplished in a second Times Film Corp. v. City of Chicago case by the corporation's asking the city for a permit to exhibit the Italian film version of the opera, Don Giovanni (Don Juan), but refusing to submit the film to the censor board for inspection. The license was denied and the case was taken to court. But the movie distributors, and the cooperating Illinois A.C.L.U., missed their guess that the time was ripe for the Supreme Court to strike down all licensing of motion pictures—missed by one vote. They gained, however, a handsome consolation prize in the form of a powerful dissenting statement by the Chief Justice, on behalf of the four-man minority.

TIMES FILM CORP. v. CITY OF CHICAGO [9]

MR. JUSTICE CLARK delivered the opinion of the Court.

. . . Admittedly, the challenged section of the ordinance imposes a previous restraint, and the broad justiciable issue is therefore present as to whether the ambit of constitutional protection includes complete and absolute freedom to exhibit, at least once, any and every kind of motion picture. It is that question alone which we decide. We have concluded that . . . Chicago's ordinance requiring the submission of films prior to their public exhibition is not, on the grounds set forth, void on its face.

. . . Petitioner claims that the nature of the film is irrelevant, and that even if this film contains the basest type of pornography, or incitement to riot, or forceful overthrow of orderly government, it may nonetheless be shown without prior submission for examination. . . . It has never been held that liberty of speech is absolute. Nor has it been suggested that all previous restraints on speech are invalid. On the contrary, in *Near* v. *Minnesota* . . . Chief Justice Hughes, in discussing the classic legal statements concern-

---

[9] 365 US 43 (1961).

ing the immunity of the press from censorship, observed that the principle forbidding previous restraint "is stated too broadly, if every such restraint is deemed to be prohibited. . . . protection even as to previous restraint is not absolutely unlimited. But the limitation has been recognized only in exceptional cases." . . . in *Roth* v. *United States* . . . we held that "in light of . . . history it is apparent that the unconditional phrasing of the First Amendment was not intended to protect every utterance." . . .

Petitioner would have us hold that the public exhibition of motion pictures must be allowed under any circumstances. The State's sole remedy, it says, is the invocation of criminal process . . . and then only after a transgression. But this position, as we have seen, is founded upon the claim of absolute privilege against prior restraint under the First Amendment—a claim without sanction in our cases. To illustrate its fallacy we need only point to one of the "exceptional cases" which Chief Justice Hughes enumerated in *Near*. . . . namely, "the primary requirements of decency [that] may be enforced against obscene publications." Moreover, we later held specifically "that obscenity is not within the area of constitutionally protected speech and press." *Roth* v. *United States*. . . .

As to what may be decided when a concrete case involving a specific standard provided by this ordinance is presented, we intimate no opinion. . . . At this time we say no more than this—that we are dealing only with motion pictures and, even as to them, only in the context of the broadside attack presented on this record.

Affirmed.

Mr. Chief Justice Warren, with whom Mr. Justice Black, Mr. Justice Douglas and Mr. Justice Brennan join, dissenting.

. . . To me, this case clearly presents the question of our approval of unlimited censorship of motion pictures before exhibition through a system of administrative licensing. Moreover, the decision presents a real danger of eventual censorship of every form of communication be it newspapers, journals, books, magazines, television, radio or public speeches. . . . in arriving at its decision the Court has interpreted our cases contrary to the intention at the time of their rendition and, in exalting the censor of motion pictures, has endangered the First and Fourteenth Amendment rights of all others engaged in the dissemination of ideas.

. . . It is not to be disputed that this Court has stated that the protection afforded First Amendment liberties from previous restraint is not absolutely unlimited. . . . But, licensing or censorship was not, at any point, considered within the "exceptional cases" discussed in the opinion in *Near*. . . . And only a few Terms ago, the Court, speaking through Mr. Justice Frankfurter, in *Kingsley Books, Inc.* v. *Brown*, . . . reaffirmed that "the limitation is the exception; it is to be closely confined so as to preclude what may fairly be deemed *licensing* or *censorship*."

Examination of the background and circumstances leading to the adoption of the First Amendment reveal the basis for the Court's steadfast observance of the proscription of licensing, censorship and previous restraint of speech. Such inquiry often begins with Blackstone's assertion: "The liberty of the press is indeed essential to the nature of a free state; but this consists in laying no previous restraints upon publications, and not in freedom from censure for criminal matter when published." . . . The objection has been that Blackstone's definition is too narrow; it had been generally conceded that the protection of the First Amendment extends *at least* to the interdiction of licensing and censorship and to the previous restraint of free speech. . . .

I hesitate to disagree with the Court's formulation of the issue before us, but, with all deference, I must insist that the question presented in this case is *not* whether a motion picture exhibitor has a constitutionally protected, "complete and absolute freedom to exhibit, at least once, any and every kind of motion picture." . . . The question here presented is whether the City of Chicago—or, for that matter, any city, any State or the Federal Government—may require all motion picture exhibitors to submit all films to a police chief, mayor or other administrative official, for licensing and censorship prior to public exhibition within the jurisdiction.

The Court does not even have before it an attempt by the city to restrain the exhibition of an allegedly "obscene" film. . . . Nor does the city contend that it is seeking to prohibit the showing of a film which will impair the "security of community life" because it acts as an incitement to "violence and the overthrow by force of orderly government." . . . The problem before us is not whether the city may forbid the exhibition of a motion picture, which, by its very showing, might in some way "inflict injury or tend to incite an immediate breach of the peace." . . .

Let it be completely clear what the Court's decision does. It . . . gives formal sanction to censorship in its purest and most far-reaching form. . . . the Court gives its assent to unlimited censorship of moving pictures through a licensing system, despite the fact that Chicago has chosen this most objectionable course to attain its goals without any apparent attempt to devise other means so as not to intrude on the constitutionally protected liberties of speech and press. . . .

As the Court recalls, in *Joseph Burstyn, Inc.* v. *Wilson* . . . it was held that motion pictures come "within the free speech and free press guaranty of the First and Fourteenth Amendments." . . . Here, once more, the Court recognized that the First Amendment's rejection of prior censorship through licensing and previous restraint is an inherent and basic principle of freedom of speech and the press. Now the Court strays from that principle; it strikes down that tenet without requiring any demonstration that this is an "exceptional case," whatever that might be, and without any indication that Chicago has sustained the "heavy burden" which was supposed to have been placed upon it. Clearly, this is neither an exceptional case nor has Chicago sustained *any* burden. . . . the Court has suggested that, in times of national emergency, the Government might impose a prior restraint upon "the publication of the sailing dates of transports or the number and location of troops." . . . But, surely this is not to suggest that the Government might require that all newspapers be submitted to a censor in order to assist it in preventing such information from reaching print. Yet in this case the Court gives its blessing to the censorship of all motion pictures in order to prevent the exhibition of those it feels to be constitutionally unprotected. . . .

It would seem idle to suppose that the Court today is unaware of the evils of the censor's basic authority, of the mischief of the system against which so many great men have waged stubborn and often precarious warfare for centuries. . . .

The censor performs free from all of the procedural safeguards afforded litigants in a court of law. . . . The likelihood of a fair and impartial trial disappears when the censor is both prosecutor and judge. There is a complete absence of rules of evidence; the fact is that there is usually no evidence at all as the system at bar vividly illustrates. How different from a judicial proceeding where a full case is presented by the litigants. . . . A member of the Chicago censor board explained that she rejected a film because "it was immoral, corrupt, indecent, against my . . . religious principles." . . . A police sergeant attached to the censor board explained, "Coarse language or anything that would be derogatory to the government—propaganda" is ruled out of foreign films. "Nothing pink or red is allowed," he added. . . . The police sergeant in charge of the censor unit has said: "Children should be allowed to see any movie that plays in Chicago. If a picture is objectionable for a child, it is objectionable period." . . . Perhaps the most powerful indictment of Chicago's licensing device is found in the fact that between the Court's decision in *Joseph Burstyn, Inc.* v. *Wilson* . . . and the filing of the petition for certiorari in 1960 in the present case, not once have the state courts upheld the censor when the exhibitor elected to appeal. . . .

This is the regimen to which the Court holds that all films must be submitted. It officially unleashes the censor and permits him to roam at will, limited only by an ordinance which contains some standards that, although concededly not before us in this case, are patently imprecise. . . . The delays in adjudication may well result in irreparable damage, both to the litigants and to the public. Vindication by the courts of *The Miracle* was not had until five years after the Chicago censor refused to license it. And then the picture was never shown in Chicago. . . . Finally, the fear of the censor by the composer of ideas acts as a substantial deterrent to the creation of new thoughts. . . . This is especially true of motion pictures due to the large financial burden that must be assumed by their producers. The censor's sword pierces deeply into the heart of free expression.

. . . The Court, in no way, explains why moving pictures should be treated differently than any other form of expression, why moving pictures should be denied the protection against censorship. . . . When pressed during oral argument, counsel for the city could make no meaningful distinction between the censorship of newspapers and motion pictures. In fact, the percentage of motion pictures dealing with social and political issues is steadily rising. The Chicago ordinance makes no exception for newsreels, documentaries, instructional and educational films or the like. All must undergo the censor's inquisition. Although it is an open question whether the impact of motion pictures is greater or less than that of other media, there is not much doubt that the exposure of television far exceeds that of the motion picture. . . .

The Court, not the petitioner, makes the "broadside attack." I would reverse the decision below.

Encouraged by the Chief Justice's opinion and by the changes in the composition of the Court that followed during the next two years, the opponents of prior censorship of films attempted still one more assault on the barricades. A Baltimore theatre manager, Ronald Freedman, exhibited the motion picture Revenge at Daybreak without first submitting it to the State Board of Censors for review and licensing. Although the film was admittedly not obscene, Freedman was convicted of violating the Maryland motion picture censorship law. On March 1, 1965, a unanimous U. S. Supreme Court reversed Freedman's conviction and, in effect, though without quite admitting it, obliterated movie censorship as we have heretofore known it (Freedman v. Maryland, No. 69).

Speaking for seven members of the Court, Mr. Justice Brennan declared that although a law is not unconstitutional simply because it requires submission of movies for censorship before public showing, the procedures must be such that the burden of proving that the film should not be shown is placed on the censors, and that actual restraint is imposed only after prompt judicial review. The Court referred to the injunctive procedure it had approved in Kingsley Books as an acceptable model to follow. In a concurring opinion, Justices Douglas and Black once again repeated their view that all motion picture censorship is unconstitutional. That the rest of the Court was in virtual agreement with them is evidenced by the fact that the procedure the majority had approved could only by the widest stretch of the term be labeled censorship. By such judicial semantics, Chief Justice Warren's Times Film dissent has become, in essence, the law of the land.

Returning to the problem of obscenity, the U. S. Supreme Court in 1962 declared still one more significant postscript to Roth when it overruled post office interference with the mailing of three magazines designed for homosexuals (Manual Enterprises v. Day, 370 US 478). Justices Harlan and Stewart, speaking for themselves rather than the Court, which could not agree on a single opinion, re-emphasized the Roth point that to be obscene, material must appeal to the prurient interest of the average audience, not just to homosexuals. But, in addition, they argued, it must be "patently offensive."

This latter criterion posed no barrier to the Supreme Court of Illinois when it decided unanimously on June 18, 1964, to find obscene both Henry Miller's book, Tropic of Cancer (Haiman* v. Morris, No. 37276), and comedian

---

* This writer had been the original plaintiff in the case, claiming illegal interference by police with his constitutional right to read. The trial judge, Samuel B. Epstein of the Superior Court of Cook County,

Lenny Bruce's performance at a Chicago night club (People State of Illinois v. Lenny Bruce, No. 37902). For, if nothing else, the language of Miller and Bruce is certainly offensive to vast numbers of people.

The justices of the Illinois high court did, however, particularly in the Tropic of Cancer case, have to reckon with a U. S. Supreme Court action just a few months earlier (Smith v. California, 375 US 259) that seemed to endorse a judgment by the California Supreme Court that this book was not obscene (Zeitlin v. Arnebergh, 31 Calif Reptr 800). Their rationale, in both Haiman and Bruce, was that California law, by prohibiting only "hard-core pornography," is not as restrictive as a state is allowed to be under the Roth decision. The Roth opinion, they argued, did not intend that only sexually stimulating communication with utterly no redeeming social importance might be found obscene. Rather, said the Illinois Supreme Court, scatological or sexual material which is revolting to the average man may be banned, even if regarded by "highly educated or sophisticated" people as containing a socially significant message.

The first amendment acting through the fourteenth amendment guards against censorship by the States of "idealogical [sic] obscenity" . . . but we feel that neither *Roth* nor *Kingsley* precludes a state from penalizing an obscene *expression* of ideas. . . . We can conclude only that defendant's mode of expressing his ideas in regard to present attitudes on contemporary social problems . . . presents a dominant theme indicating a morbid interest in sex which so overbalances the commentary presented, that the performance, when viewed as a whole, must be held obscene . . . (*People State of Illinois v. Lenny Bruce*).

Four days after these Illinois opinions, the U. S. Supreme Court announced two decisions which undermined the

---

had ruled in our favor: "Let the parents control the reading matter of their children; let the tastes of the readers determine what may or may not be read; let each reader be his own censor; but let not the government or the courts dictate the reading matter of a free people."

position taken by the Illinois Supreme Court. One was a reversal, without opinion, of a Florida judgment that Tropic of Cancer was obscene (Grove Press v. Gerstein, 378 US 577). The other overturned, 6-3, an obscenity conviction of a theater manager in Cleveland Heights, Ohio, for having exhibited a French film, The Lovers.

Justice Brennan, in his opinion in the latter case, attempted to clarify the Roth decision. In so doing, he directly contradicted the interpretation placed on it by Illinois. Justices Black and Douglas, concurring in the decision, continued to hold out for the more libertarian position of their Roth dissent. Chief Justice Warren, dissenting, not only disputed Justice Brennan's definition of "contemporary community standards," but would have left the whole matter to the Ohio courts.

JACOBELLIS v. OHIO [10]

MR. JUSTICE BRENNAN announced the judgment of the Court and delivered an opinion in which MR. JUSTICE GOLDBERG joins.

. . . The question of the proper standard for making this determination has been the subject of much discussion and controversy since our decision in *Roth-Alberts* seven years ago. Recognizing that the test for obscenity enunciated there . . . is not perfect, we think any substitute would raise equally difficult problems, and we therefore adhere to that standard. We would reiterate, however, our recognition in *Roth* that obscenity is excluded from the constitutional protection only because it is "utterly without redeeming social importance," and that "the portrayal of sex, e.g., in art, literature, and scientific works, is not itself sufficient reason to deny material the constitutional protection of freedom of speech and press." . . . It follows that material dealing with sex in a manner that advocates ideas . . . or that has literary or scientific or artistic value or any other form of social importance, may not be branded as obscenity and denied the constitutional protection. Nor may the constitutional status of the material be

---

[10] 378 US 184 (1964).

made to turn on a "weighing" of its social importance against its prurient appeal, for a work cannot be proscribed unless it is "utterly" without social importance. . . .

It has been suggested that the "contemporary community standards" aspect of the *Roth* test implies a determination of the constitutional question of obscenity in each case by the standards of the particular local community from which the case arises. This is an incorrect reading of *Roth*. The concept of "contemporary community standards" was first expressed by Judge Learned Hand in *United States* v. *Kennerley*. . . . It seems clear that . . . Judge Hand was referring not to state and local "communities," but rather to "the community" in the sense of "society at large; . . . the public, or people in general." Thus he recognized that under his standard the concept of obscenity would have "a varying meaning from time to time"—not from county to county, or town to town.

We do not see how any "local" definition of the "community" could properly be employed in delineating the area of expression that is protected by the Federal Constitution. . . .

It is true that local communities throughout the land are in fact diverse, and that in cases such as this one the Court is confronted with the task of reconciling the rights of such communities with the rights of individuals. Communities vary, however, in many respects other than their toleration of alleged obscenity, and such variances have never been considered to require or justify a varying standard for application of the Federal Constitution. . . . We thus affirm the position taken in *Roth* to the effect that the constitutional status of an allegedly obscene work must be determined on the basis of a national standard. It is, after all, a national Constitution we are expounding.

MR. JUSTICE STEWART, concurring.

. . . I have reached the conclusion, which I think is confirmed at least by negative implication in the Court's decisions since *Roth* and *Alberts*, that under the First and Fourteenth Amendments criminal laws in this area are constitutionally limited to hard-core pornography. I shall not today attempt further to define the kinds of material I understand to be embraced within that short-hand description; and perhaps I could never succeed in intelligibly doing so. But I know it when I see it, and the motion picture involved in this case is not that.

THE CHIEF JUSTICE, with whom MR. JUSTICE CLARK joins, dissenting.

. . . It is my belief that when the Court said in *Roth* that obscenity is to be defined by reference to "community standards," it meant community standards—not a national standard, as is sometimes argued. I believe that there is no provable "national standard," and perhaps there should be none. At all events, this Court has not been able to enunciate one, and it would be unreasonable to expect local courts to divine one. It is said that such a "community" approach may well result in material being proscribed as obscene in one community but not in another, and, in all probability, that is true. But communities throughout the nation are in fact diverse, and it must be remembered that, in cases such as this one, the Court is confronted with the task of reconciling rights of the diverse communities within our society and of individuals.

Although the Court, in Jacobellis, was too divided in its reasons for overturning the conviction to agree on a single majority opinion, Justice Brennan's interpretation of the Roth decision carried with it the authority not only of its lead position but of his earlier authorship of Roth itself. Apparently deferring to his views as well as the Court's decision, the Supreme Court of Illinois, two weeks later, took a most unusual action. On its own initiative it withdrew its opinion in Haiman v. Morris, vacated its own judgment, and ordered Judge Epstein's lower court opinion affirmed. Furthermore, it scheduled the Lenny Bruce case for rehearing, in the light of Jacobellis, during its next term, and in November, 1964, reversed that conviction as well.

———————◆———————

As the Supreme Court has drawn an increasingly narrow boundary around what may be legally proscribed as obscene, community vigilantes have steadily increased the scope and variety of their extra-legal pressures. On occasion they have gone so far as to violate the law themselves. Two cases, a decade apart, are of particular note. The first, in 1953, concerned the actions of the police chief of Youngstown, Ohio. In a series of communications with a local bookdealer, Chief Allen had presented a list of over 100 books which he considered obscene and demanded be withdrawn from sale. No move was ever taken by him to obtain a court determination of obscenity or to initiate any other legal action. One of the publishers whose books were in question went to the federal district court and won an injunction against Allen's extra-legal activities (New American Library v. Allen, 114 F Supp 823). The decision was not appealed.

In 1963, the U. S. Supreme Court received on appeal a similar case from the State of Rhode Island. There the legislature had established a state Commission to Encourage Morality in Youth, which engaged in the business of compiling lists of objectionable publications and sending them to booksellers with a demand that they be removed from the shelves. The Supreme Court, 8-1, found these activities in violation of the First Amendment and sustained an injunction (Bantam Books v. Sullivan, 372 US 58). Said Justice Brennan for the majority:

> We are not the first court to look through forms to substance and recognize that informal censorship may sufficiently inhibit the circulation of publications to warrant injunctive relief.

These decisions leave untouched, of course, the activities of private groups, such as the Citizens for Decent Literature committees which have been springing up with increasing frequency around the country. So long as such groups restrict themselves to persuasion, eschewing organized economic coercion or alliances with the power of the state, their speech too is entitled to the protections of the First Amendment. If they overstep these bounds they may be stopped by the courts, as was the Boston Watch and Ward Society back in 1926 when it engaged in a program of threatening to instigate prosecutions against magazine distributors if they failed to withdraw from circulation items on the society's list of disapproved publications (American Mercury, Inc. v. Chase et al., 13 F 2d 224).

———————◆———————

While films and books have been so heavily engaged in litigation, radio and television have remained relatively untouched by law. In part this has been due to a highly cautious policy of self-censorship on the part of broadcasters and perhaps in part to fear of possible license withdrawal by the Federal Communications Commission. Station managers exercise great vigilance, for example, concerning the use of off-color language, and at least one of the major networks has gone so far as to exclude from its channels all known Communists, whether intending to appear in the role of party spokesmen or as entertainers. In a society like ours, where radio and television are probably the most significant media of public communication, we cannot pretend to have dealt adequately with the problems of freedom of speech without concerning ourselves with the manner in which controls are exercised over the airwaves. But thus far there has been little governmental or legal involvement in these matters. Aside from some occasional disputes over the constitutionality of its "Fairness Doctrine," the first time that the Federal Communications Commission made a decision about which serious freedom of speech questions were raised was in 1962, when an application for license renewal was denied to Station WDKD of Kingstree, South Carolina (Palmetto Broadcasting Company, 33 FCC 250).

One of the grounds on which this action was based was that a disk jockey named Charlie Walker, whose programs constituted as much as 25 per cent of the broadcast day, consistently used material described as "coarse, vulgar, suggestive, and susceptible of indecent, double meaning" and "flagrantly offensive . . . by any standard." But the Commission also made clear that it regarded this as a most unusual case, involving many considerations which demonstrated that the station was not being operated in the public interest, as required by F.C.C. regulations.

The Commission had a further opportunity to clarify its position on free speech matters when, at the beginning of

1964, it was called upon to decide another controversial case of license renewal, as a result of complaints received against a series of programs broadcast by the Pacifica Foundation.

Federal Communications Commission:[11]

. . . The principal complaints are concerned with five programs: (i) a December 12, 1959 broadcast over KPFA, at 10 P.M., of certain poems by Lawrence Ferlinghetti (read by the poet himself); (ii) *The Zoo Story,* a recording of the Edward Albee play broadcast over KPFK at 11 P.M., January 13, 1963; (iii) *Live and Let Live,* a program broadcast over KPFK at 10:15 P.M. on January 15, 1963, in which eight homosexuals discussed their attitudes and problems; (iv) a program broadcast over KPFA at 7:15 P.M. on January 28, 1963, in which the poem, *Ballad of the Despairing Husband,* was read by the author Robert Creeley; and (v) *The Kid,* a program broadcast at 11 P.M. on January 8, 1963, over KPFA, which consisted of readings by Edward Pomerantz from his unfinished novel of the same name. The complaints charge that these programs were offensive or "filthy" in nature. . . .

There is, we think, no question but that the broadcasts of the programs, *The Zoo Story, Live and Let Live,* and *The Kid,* lay well within the licensee's judgment under the public interest standard. The situation here stands on an entirely different footing than *Palmetto, supra,* where the licensee had devoted a substantial period of his broadcast day to material which we found to be patently offensive— however much we weighted that standard in the licensee's favor—and as to which programming the licensee himself never asserted that it was not offensive or vulgar, *or that it served the needs of his area or had any redeeming features.* In this case, Pacifica has stated its judgment that the three above-cited programs served the public interests and specifically, the needs and interests of its listening public. Thus, it has pointed out that in its judgment, *The Zoo Story* is a "serious work of drama" by an eminent and

---

[11] *Memorandum Opinion and Order,* January 22, 1964, 64-43.

"provocative playwright"—that it is "an honest and courageous play" which Americans "who do not live near
Broadway ought to have the opportunity to hear and experience. . . ." Similarly, as to *The Kid*, Pacifica states, with
supporting authority, that Mr. Pomerantz is an author who
has obtained notable recognition for his writings and whose
readings from his unfinished novel were fully in the public
interest as a serious work meriting the attention of its listeners; Pacifica further states that prior to broadcast, the
tape was auditioned by one of its employees who edited out
two phrases because they did not meet Pacifica's broadcast
standards of good taste; and that while "certain minor
swear words are used, . . . these fit well within the context
of the material being read and conform to the standards of acceptability of reasonably intelligent listeners." Finally, as to the program, *Live and Let Live*, Pacifica states
that "so long as the program is handled in good taste, there
is no reason why subjects like homosexuality should not be
discussed on the air"; and that it "conscientiously believes
that the American people will be better off as a result of
hearing a constructive discussion of the problem rather
than leaving the subject to ignorance and silence."

We recognize that as shown by the complaints here,
such provocative programming as here involved may offend
some listeners. But this does not mean that those offended
have the right, through the Commission's licensing power,
to rule such programming off the airwaves. Were this the
case, only the wholly inoffensive, the bland, could gain access to the radio microphone or TV camera. No such
drastic curtailment can be countenanced under the Constitution, the Communications Act, or the Commission's
policy, which has consistently sought to insure "the maintenance of radio and television as a medium of freedom of
speech and freedom of expression for the people of the Nation as a whole" (*Editorializing Report*, 13 F.C.C. 1246,
1248). In saying this, we do not mean to indicate that
those who have complained about the foregoing programs
are in the wrong as to the worth of these programs and
should listen to them. This is a matter solely for determination by the individual listeners. Our function, we stress, is

not to pass on the merits of the program—to commend or to frown. Rather . . . it is the very limited one of assaying, at the time of renewal, whether the licensee's programming, on an overall basis, has been in the public interest and, in the context of this issue, whether he has made programming judgments reasonably related to the public interest. This does not pose a close question in the case: Pacifica's judgments as to the above programs clearly fall within the very great discretion which the Act wisely vests in the licensee. In this connection, we also note that Pacifica took into account the nature of the broadcast medium when it scheduled such programming for the late evening hours (after 10 P.M., when the number of children in the listening audience is at a minimum).

As to the Ferlinghetti and Creeley programs, the licensee asserts that in both instances, some passages did not measure up to "Pacifica's own standards of good taste." Thus, it states that it did not carefully screen the Ferlinghetti tape to see if it met its standards "because it relied upon Mr. Ferlinghetti's national reputation and also upon the fact that the tape came to it from a reputable FM station." It acknowledges that this was a mistake in its procedures and states that "in the future Pacifica will make its own review of all broadcasts. . . ." With respect to the Creeley passage (i.e., the poem, *Ballad of a Despairing Husband*), Pacifica again states that in its judgment it should not have been broadcast. It "does not excuse the broadcast of the poem in question" but it does explain how the poem "slipped by" KPFA's Drama and Literature Editor who auditioned the tape. It points out that prior to the offending poem, Mr. Creeley, who "has a rather flat, monotonous voice," read eighteen other perfectly acceptable poems— and that the station's editor was so lulled thereby that he did not catch the few offensive words on the nineteenth poem. It also points out that each of the nine poems which followed was again perfectly acceptable, and that before re-broadcasting the poem on its Los Angeles station, it deleted the objectionable verse.

In view of the foregoing, we find no impediment to renewal on this score. We are dealing with two isolated errors in the licensee's application of its own standards—one in 1959 and the other in 1963. The explanations given for these two errors are credible. Therefore, even assuming, *arguendo*, that the broadcasts were inconsistent with the public interest standard, it is clear that no unfavorable action upon the renewal applications is called for. The standard of public interest is not so rigid that an honest mistake or error on the part of a licensee results in drastic action against him where his overall record demonstrates a reasonable effort to serve the needs and interests of his community. . . . Here again, this case contrasts sharply with *Palmetto* where instead of two isolated instances, years apart, we found that the patently offensive material was broadcast for a substantial period of the station's broadcast day for many years.

We find, therefore, that the programming matters raised with respect to the Pacifica renewals pose no bar to a grant of renewal.* Our holding, as is true of all such holdings in this sensitive area, is necessarily based on, and limited to, the facts of the particular case. But we have tried to stress here, as in *Palmetto*, an underlying policy—that the licensee's judgment in this freedom of speech area is entitled to very great weight and that the Commission, under the public interest standard, will take action against the licensee at the time of renewal only where the facts of the particular case, established in a hearing record, flagrantly call for such action. We have done so because we are charged under the Act with "promoting the larger and more effective use of radio in the public interest" (Section 303(g)), and obviously, in the discharge of that responsibility, must take every precaution to avoid inhibiting broadcast licensees'

---

* One other programming aspect deserves emphasis. Complaint has also been made concerning Pacifica's presentation of "far-left" programming. Pacifica has stated that it follows a policy of presenting programs covering the widest range of the political or controversial issue spectrum —from the members of the Communist Party on the left to members of the John Birch Society on the right. Again, we point out that such a policy (which must, of course, be carried out consistently with the requirements of the fairness doctrine) is within the licensee's area of programming judgment.

efforts at experimenting or diversifying their programming. Such diversity of programming has been the goal of many Commission policies (e.g., multiple ownership, development of UHF, the fairness doctrine). Clearly, the Commission must remain faithful to that goal in discharging its functions in the action area of programming itself.

———————◆———————

So much for the position of law-enforcing bodies on artistic expression and the problem of public morality. We now turn to the community arena where the contending positions also vie for acceptance. First, let us examine the libertarian side of the argument.

American Civil Liberties Union:[12]

. . . the American Civil Liberties Union declared on May 28, 1962, that "the constitutional guarantees of free speech apply to all expression."

The ACLU's Board of Directors . . . asserted in a policy statement its belief that "limitations of expression on the ground of obscenity are unconstitutional."

But, the ACLU said, if obscenity laws are invoked prosecutions should be based on clear proof that the material would cause, "in a normal adult, behavior which has validly been made criminal by statute. A special exception would be permissible if the target group of the allegedly obscene material were children. In these cases the standard to be applied in judging such material should be whether its effect on children would lead to behavior that would violate a criminal statute. . . .

"Even under the Supreme Court's 1957 definition of obscenity in the *Roth* case—'whether to the average person, applying community standards, the dominant theme of the material taken as a whole appeals to prurient interest'— courts and juries continue to differ over what constitutes obscenity, often including books which have won worldwide acclaim. This is only natural since individual judgments, whether of a book, a magazine, a film, a play or a

_____
[12] Excerpts from statement of March, 1963.

painting, are inevitably subjective and personal. What may strike one man as pornographic may be a matter of complete indifference to another. What may be offensive to one person may be great art to another person. And frequently such individual judgments condemn most severely only controversial expression—the very kind of speech for whose protection the First Amendment was written." . . .

"We do not say that every book or publication carries ideas of importance to the community, but we do believe that every act of deciding what should be barred carries with it danger to the community. Because of the special need in a free society to guard against the stifling effect of censorship no ban should be placed on allegedly obscene material, even though much material may be intensely disliked by many persons.

"This is never a popular position but we are convinced that it is the right one. The seeds of censorship have been planted in far too many areas of American life, usually with the intention of curing an evil. But rarely does the evil recede when censorship is imposed. The causes of such social problems as juvenile delinquency, which often prompt demands for censorship, are much deeper. Moreover, banning any expression only boosts interest in it and results in wider circulation of the offensive material. The experience of the Prohibition Days proved this." . . .

This standard follows the Union's traditional "clear and present danger" position under which free speech may be limited, the statement emphasized. If accepted, prosecutions would at least relate to "some definable criteria in an admittedly murky field. The mounting pressure for removal of offensive books and other materials in recent years has had as its basis the assumption that there is a clear connection between such material and anti-social behavior; actually, there is a wide difference of opinion among experts on what influences such material may have. The standard we propose would bring the issue of alleged obscenity into the realm of reality where in a court of law it can be considered in the context of calm, rational evaluation of evidence rather than an emotional insistence upon 'action' against 'dirty books.' The requirement of proof that the particular material would cause criminal behavior may seem difficult to meet. But there is no lazy man's way of preserving a cherished First Amendment guarantee. We must insist on strict standards of proof before such a vital right as freedom of expression may be curbed." . . .

John Ciardi:[13]

. . . nothing suggests sex more movingly than a girl to a boy and a boy to a girl. And since both seem to be in plentiful supply, that suggestion will, I submit, be made. The response that follows, dear mother and dad, will follow from whatever moral standards you have implanted in your young.

You cannot ask the community to do for your child by censorship what you have not done for him by example. Hide the world from him and he will go to the world in ignorance. Treat sex as a furtive thing and he will probably go to it furtively. . . . I know of no moral standards that *can* be damaged by being given a basis in fact.

On the issue of obscenity, the usually libertarian Professor Chafee found himself uncomfortably attempting to straddle the middle of the road.

Zechariah Chafee, Jr.:[14]

The true explanation is that profanity and indecent talk and pictures, which do not form an essential part of any exposition of ideas, have a very slight social value as a step toward truth, which is clearly outweighed by the social interests in order, morality, the training of the young, and the peace of mind of those who hear and see. Words of this type offer little opportunity for the usual process of counter-argument. The harm is done as soon as they are communicated, or is liable to follow almost immediately in the form

---

[13] Reprinted by permission of the publisher from John Ciardi, "Manner of Speaking," *Saturday Review* (August 10, 1963), p. 16.

[14] Reprinted by permission of the publishers from Zechariah Chafee, Jr., *Free Speech in the United States* (Cambridge, Mass.: Harvard University Press), pp. 150-55. Copyright, 1941, by the President and Fellows of Harvard College.

of retaliatory violence. The only sound explanation of the punishment of obscenity and profanity is that the words are criminal, not because of the ideas they communicate, but like acts because of their immediate consequences to the five senses. The man who swears in a street car is as much of a nuisance as the man who smokes there. . . . The man who talks scurrilously about the flag commits a crime, not because the implications of his ideas tend to weaken the Federal Government, but because the effect resembles that of an injurious act such as trampling on the flag, which would be a public nuisance and a breach of the peace. . . .

This breach of the peace theory is peculiarly liable to abuse when applied against unpopular expressions and practices. It makes a man a criminal simply because his neighbors have no self-control and cannot refrain from violence. The *reductio ad absurdum* of this theory was the imprisonment of Joseph Palmer, one of Bronson Alcott's fellow-settlers at "Fruitlands," not because he was a communist, but because he persisted in wearing such a long beard that people kept mobbing him, until law and order were maintained by shutting him up. A man does not become a criminal because someone else assaults him, unless his own conduct is in itself illegal or may be reasonably considered a direct provocation to violence.

Thus all these crimes of injurious words must be kept within very narrow limits if they are not to give excessive opportunities for outlawing heterodox ideas.

At the opposite pole from the American Civil Liberties Union and its supporters stands the traditional position of the Roman Catholic Church and its unofficial arm in America, the Legion of Decency.

Harold C. Gardiner, S.J.: [15]

Canon Law itself does not define the obscene. . . . To discover this we have to go to authoritative interpreta-

---

[15] Reprinted by permission of the publishers from Harold C. Gardiner, S.J., *Catholic Viewpoint on Censorship*, pp. 63-66, 98-102. Copyright © 1958, 1961 by Doubleday & Company, Inc.

tions. . . . It consists in the intrinsic tendency or bent of the work to arouse sexual passion, or, to put it more concretely, the motions of the genital apparatus which are preparatory to the complete act of sexual union. It must be noted that a particular work—the book, the statue, and so on—may not always and in all circumstances so arouse this or that individual. . . . It is not so much a matter of the individual's own reaction here and now as to the nature of the work under consideration. And it must be the *intrinsic* nature of the work, not an accidental circumstance. So, for example, one of perverse moral character or abnormal sexual excitability might possibly be sexually aroused by stroking a rose petal or a piece of velvet, but no one would call either object obscene.

Further, the sexual arousement need not actually follow the contemplation of the object that is obscene. In Catholic sex morality, the deliberate arousal of sexual thoughts that are of their nature destined to be preparatory to sexual stimulation and the complete act is of itself a serious sin. . . .

This is called by the theologians "venereal pleasure." . . . If the work is *not* such a kind, it may, indeed, be vulgar, disgusting, crude, unpleasant, what you will—but it will *not* be, in the strict sense which Canon Law obliges us to apply, obscene. Let us repeat, this interpretation is by no means an apology or excuse for vulgar and disgusting works, and Catholic groups are well within their moral and legal rights when they protest the presence of such stuff for general consumption. But it is a reminder that, since a restriction of human liberty is here at stake, that liberty must be and can be restricted only as far as is necessary for the attainment of a higher good. Indulgence in vulgarity may or may not be a sin, depending on circumstances; indulgence in obscenity is always a sin, and freedom from temptation to that sin is the higher good the law envisions and protects.

The following remarks were made by Mrs. James F. Looram, chairman of the Motion Picture Department of the International Confederation of Catholic Alumnae, at the twentieth convention of the IFCA held at St. Paul on August 26, 1955. The IFCA has supplied the Legion's [Legion of Decency] reviewing staff from the very start. . . . "The *theme* of a movie is what largely determines its morality. . . . It is the answer given rather than the problem presented that constitutes the morality of the theme as such. If it were not for this, very few real dilemmas of life could be presented at all, and no stories of repentance after wrongdoing.

"In cases where the decision itself is immoral, the writer may still have a moral theme if he created dislike instead of sympathy for the leading character, and shows how the false decision leads to tragedy and retribution, such as in *Macbeth*.

"The reviewer notes whether there is reform, regeneration, punishment, retribution: in other words—adequate moral compensation. . . . She must be meticulously careful to note if sin is presented as a mistake or as a shameful transgression. . . .

"Sin must always be shown for what it is, not a mistake but a shameful transgression. . . .

"Of course, our reviewers are not infallible. Until the baseball umpire calls all the plays to the satisfaction of everyone on the teams and in the stands, we cannot expect to be infallible for, like the umpire, we are human. . . ."

. . . It cannot be denied that from time to time the Legion [of Decency] is *asked* (it can make no demands) by producers to give an opinion on a script in process; changes have occasionally been made when a producer has come for advice. But this is certainly no more "prior censorship" than would be the guidance asked for and taken by a young writer who requested an Ernest Hemingway to read and criticize his manuscript.

Father Gardiner's closing analogy warrants careful examination. To be sure, the Legion of Decency cannot fairly be accused of prior restraint in the legal sense. But whether the awareness of its powerful extra-legal sanctions is in the same category as spontaneously sought advice from a famous critic is open to question. A similar question may, indeed, be raised about the movie industry's own "voluntary" and "self-imposed" Production Code Authority, which grants or denies to a film the industry's seal of approval. To an individual producer who may wish to violate the code, the knowledge that a film without the seal of approval cannot be shown on any U. S. military base may constitute a somewhat more than self-imposed restraint.

The desire of a distributor of artistic expression—be he a movie or play producer, or a bookseller—to have advance assurance that his activities will not lose him money or get him into trouble with the law is understandable. The following excerpt, in discussing the licensing of plays in London, England, states the position well.

George Bernard Shaw:[16]

The manager of a theatre is a man of business. He is not an expert in politics, religion, art, literature, philosophy, or law. . . . by no means . . . qualified to judge whether a play is safe from prosecution or not. He may not understand it, may not like it, may not know what the author is driving at, may have no knowledge of the ethical, political, and sectarian controversies which may form the intellectual fabric of the play. . . . Yet if he produces the play he is legally responsible just as if he had written it himself. Without protection he may find himself in the dock answering a charge of blasphemous libel, seditious libel, obscene libel, or all three together. . . . His sole refuge is the opinion of the Examiner of Plays, his sole protection the licence of the Lord Chamberlain. A refusal to license does not hurt him, because he can produce another play: it is the author who suffers. The granting of the licence practically places him above the law; for though it may be legally possible to prosecute a licensed play, nobody ever dreams of doing it. . . .

---

[16] Reprinted by permission of the Public Trustee and the Society of Authors from George Bernard Shaw, "Preface on the Censorship," in *The Shewing-Up of Blanco Posnet* (New York: Brentano's, 1913), pp. 11-13.

The censorship, then, provides the manager, at the negligible premium of two guineas per play, with an effective insurance against the author getting him into trouble, and a complete relief from all conscientious responsibility for the character of the entertainment at his theatre. Under such circumstances, managers would be more than human if they did not regard the censorship as their most valuable privilege.

To deal with this problem in the United States, Professor Chafee has suggested the possibility of establishing by law a system of "play juries," whose function would be to view a production in advance of its opening and issue a declaratory judgment regarding its possible indecency. If approved by the jury, the play would be safe from prosecution. If not, the producer could, if he wanted to, withdraw it without being hurt. (Free Speech in the United States, 531 ff.) To follow such a proposal, it appears, would take us back once again to the philosophy that the audience reaction of "typical" men and women should be the test of the permissible bounds of freedom of speech.

We have seen, in the words of Father Gardiner, the traditional viewpoint of the Catholic Church. But that institution, like all others, has its dissenters, as exemplified by the vigorous young Swiss theologian, Father Hans Kung, who toured America in 1963 advocating, among other things, the abolition of the Catholic Index of Prohibited Books. Another spokesman for the liberal wing of Catholicism is a former teacher of speech and now well-known drama critic for the New York Herald Tribune.

Walter Kerr: [17]

We have said that the authorized censor must, because of the peculiar duty with which he is charged, be indiffer-

---

[17] Reprinted by permission of the National Catholic Educational Association from Walter Kerr, *Criticism and Censorship* (Milwaukee: The Bruce Publishing Company), pp. 51-55, 81-85. Copyright, 1956, by the National Catholic Educational Association. Originally presented as a lecture at Trinity College in 1954.

ent to the needs and nature of art. Turn the social mass
into a hydraheaded censor and you are left with an entire
society that is indifferent to the needs and nature of
art. . . . Thus the aesthetic criteria that the authorized
censor has reluctantly put aside as irrelevant to his peculiar
task are now lightly and even cheerfully put aside by the
entire community. Art ceases to have laws of its own, even
a character of its own. In the popular mind it becomes an
appendage to morals. . . . The result is—necessarily—a
low level of taste in the community, perhaps the disappear-
ance of taste altogether. The community no longer has any
means at its disposal for distinguishing one piece of work
from another provided both subscribe to the same moral
code. A vulgar virgin is as good as a sensitively conceived
virgin; the only thing that matters is that it is a virgin.

. . . The truth of the matter is that none of us—not
even the most passionate opponent of the very principle of
censorship—really cares what happens to bad art. If the
work is aesthetically poor, we don't honestly care what
the censor does with it, or what anyone else does with it.
The world can wrap fish with it—as it most certainly will—
and we're not going to mind.

The essential fear that nags at the critical mind whenever it is confronted by censorship is the fear that *good* art
will be lost. This is a valid, reasonable fear. The possibility
is a real possibility. There is the further fear, and the further possibility, that in an atmosphere dominated by widespread, habitual, amateur censorship good art will never
even be produced, let alone lost.

. . . the health of society, it must be remembered, does
not come from negative, protective acts alone. Caution in
itself does not guarantee a man safe and sound passage
through a complex world. . . . Health is as much the result of positive, vigorously creative acts as it is of prudential
acts. . . . It was in speaking, briefly, of the theater that
St. Thomas said ". . . No man can exist without pleasure,
and when he cannot enjoy the pleasures of the spirit he
seeks those of the flesh." . . .

No man can *exist* without pleasure; the Puritan shrivels
within himself and loses a part of his very being. A society

committed to a Puritan habit of thought, or even a semi-Puritan habit of thought, is not a living society but a half-fossilized one. . . . Bundling up won't do the job all by itself; exercise is essential. As Catholics, we've been doing a lot of bundling up and taking very little exercise. American society as a whole is not, at the moment, in very trim shape. If we have, or are on the way to having, a society that is partially sick, it is because very few of us have learned how to be properly playful.

The diffusion of the censorial mind over the whole community is, to be blunt about it, a sign of sickness.

Mr. Kerr, though warning of censorial excesses, does not believe that censorship can or should be entirely abandoned. Nor does the author of the following review.

John E. Coons:[18]

Even if the ideal is commendable, is it really practical to plump for the complete abolition of censorship? Perhaps after all we should recognize the extreme durability of the censoring impulse in this area. Its antiquity is sometimes astonishing. Since fallen Adam donned the fig leaf there have been censors. Until doomsday there will be censors. The Supreme Court has granted them its benison. Their elimination is impossible. Their transfiguration is at least conceivable. Shaw once argued that no one really knows whether Christianity will work or not, because it has never been tried. With apologies to that doughty old freespeaker, we might wonder analogically whether a rational censorship of obscenity has even been attempted. Not in our age, certainly, where we observe daily the cheerful and witless assassination by boards of housewives and police commissioners of an infinite variety of material—mostly, but not all, trivia. Is this the immutable character of censorship or but a caricature? Do censors become fools before or after their

---

[18] Reprinted by special permission of Northwestern University School of Law from John E. Coons' book review of Richard McKeon, Robert K. Merton, and Walter Gellhorn, *The Freedom to Read,* 53 *Northwestern University Law Review* 127 (1958), pp. 131-32. Copyright © 1958 by Northwestern University School of Law.

appointment? This last is not an idle question. If . . .
censors are generally selected from persons temperamen-
tally and educationally unsuited, their blunders may indicate nothing more than their own vacuity. They do not
necessarily support the thesis that the censor's office is by
nature a pest house. It would be fascinating to watch the
results of a concerted liberal attempt to reform rather than
simply to eradicate censorship, a movement in which liberals would be willing to accept—indeed would seek—an official censoring responsibility. Maybe the only thing that
censorship lacks in order to be wearing laurel instead of
straws in its hair is a new breed of censor who loves literature, art, and freedom and who, to the same degree, de-
spises the necessity for his job. Such a man would censor
only material void even of pretensions to idea content and
then only as a painful last resort. . . . No doubt this is too
sensible a solution to be realistic, but if liberals believed it,
it could come true.

But the Coons argument for a liberal and enlightened
censorship was anticipated and answered long ago.

George Bernard Shaw:[19]

. . . Indifference to the larger issues of a theatrical performance could not be safely predicated of an enlightened
censorship. Such a censorship might be more liberal in its
toleration of matters which are only objected to on the
ground that they are not usually discussed in general social
conversation or in the presence of children; but it would
presumably have a far deeper insight to and concern for the
real ethical tendency of the play. For instance, had it been
in existence during the last quarter of a century, it would
have perceived that those plays of Ibsen's which have been
licensed without question are fundamentally immoral to an
altogether extraordinary degree. Every one of them is a

---

[19] Reprinted by permission of the Public Trustee and The Society of
Authors from George Bernard Shaw, "Preface on the Censorship," in
The Shewing-Up of Blanco Posnet (New York: Brentano's, 1913), pp.
49-50.

deliberate act of war on society as at present constituted.
. . . Now you cannot license work of that sort without
making yourself responsible for it. The Lord Chamberlain
accepted the responsibility because he did not understand
it or concern himself about it. But what really enlightened
and conscientious official dare take such a responsibility? . . .

We may, therefore, conclude that the more enlightened
a censorship is, the worse it would serve us. The Lord
Chamberlain, an obviously unenlightened Censor, prohibits Ghosts and licenses all the rest of Ibsen's plays. An enlightened censorship would possibly license Ghosts; but it
would certainly suppress many of the other plays. . . .
Under the Lord Chamberlain, we can smuggle a good
deal of immoral drama, and almost as much coarsely vulgar
and furtively lascivious drama as we like. Under a college of
cardinals, or bishops, or judges, or any other conceivable
form of experts in morals, philosophy, religion, or politics,
we should get little except stagnant mediocrity.

QUESTIONS FOR DISCUSSION

1. In what respect is Judge Frank (in Roth) more of a
libertarian than Judge Bok (in Gordon)? In what respect
are they both more libertarian than the U. S. Supreme
Court majority in Roth?

2. What is the major significance of Burstyn? Of Kingsley
International Pictures?

3. What, if any, effective answer can be made to the position taken by Justices Douglas and Black in Superior Films

and Chief Justice Warren in Times Film that movie censorship per se is unconstitutional?

4. How did the use of an injunction in Near differ from that in Kingsley Books? Would the injunctive method be a reasonable alternative to censorship boards in the area of movies, and would Chief Justice Warren approve?

5. Aside from the definition of obscenity which has served as the leading precedent in this field, of what other major significance to First Amendment doctrine was the majority opinion in Roth?

6. One can agree wholeheartedly with the F.C.C. decisions in Palmetto Broadcasting Company and Pacifica Foundation and still be concerned about their possible ramifications? How might this be so?

7. What justification can be offered for banning obscenity (as defined in Roth) while permitting scatology, profanity, and the portrayal of violence? Can as good or better an argument be made for permitting obscenity, scatology, and profanity and prohibiting the portrayal of violence? Or some other combination?

8. Can a valid distinction be maintained between communication which has redeeming social importance and that which does not? If so, how can it be done?

9. On what, if any, basis is our society justified in maintaining greater government control over radio and television than other media of communication?

10. Should it be permissible for a local Citizens Committee for Decent Literature to threaten a neighborhood drug store owner with a boycott if he does not remove specified publications from his newsstand?

4

Provocation, Heresy, Obscenity: Strands of the Same Fabric?

"Whose foot is to be the measure to which ours
are all to be cut or stretched?"
—Thomas Jefferson,
Letter to Dufief

As one studies the cases and questions presented in the
preceding chapters he cannot help but be struck by the re-
curring themes to be found there. So interrelated do issues
appear that one wonders if we are dealing with three dis-
tinguishable areas of communication or whether problems
in freedom of speech possess a unitary quality which is,
after all, implied by the brief and simple phraseology of the
First Amendment.

To raise this question is to pose a problem that has not
yet been resolved either by our highest court or by scholars
of the subject. Whether "the freedom of speech" that Congress and the States are forbidden by the Bill of Rights to
abridge means all speech, or only political speech, or socially useful speech, or speech that does not infringe on
other rights, or only speech that a majority acting through
due process decides to allow, is still a matter of wide dispute. Although we need not be bound in this by what the
Founding Fathers may have meant, their intentions are
inevitably influential. Thus, many writers have been concerned with interpreting their motives. Others have attempted to apply some kind of "rule of reason" and thus

to find a position which seems to accommodate both the ideals we espouse and pragmatic realities. Still others, believing that the writers of the First Amendment meant literally what they said when they wrote that Congress shall make no law abridging the freedom of speech, have sought to define freedom of speech in such a way as to make a literal reading of the "no law" phrase viable.

We can best understand this particular controversy, and perhaps find for ourselves a way toward its resolution, by turning beyond particular cases and court decisions and examining the views of various scholars and essayists who have expressed themselves upon it.

Zechariah Chafee, Jr.:[1]

The First Amendment protects two kinds of interests in free speech. There is an individual interest, the need of many men to express their opinions on matters vital to them if life is to be worth living, and a social interest in the attainment of truth, so that the country may not only adopt the wisest course of action but carry it out in the wisest way. This social interest is especially important in war time. . . . Truth can be sifted out from falsehood only if the government is vigorously and constantly cross-examined. . . . Legal proceedings prove that an opponent makes the best cross-examiner. Consequently it is a disastrous mistake to limit criticism to those who favor the war. Men bitterly hostile to it may point out evils in its management like the secret treaties, which its supporters have been too busy to unearth. . . .

The great trouble with most judicial construction of the Espionage Act is that this social interest has been ignored and free speech has been regarded as merely an individual interest, which must readily give way like other personal desires the moment it interferes with the social interest in national safety. . . .

---

[1] Reprinted by permission of the publishers from Zechariah Chafee, Jr., *Free Speech in the United States* (Cambridge, Mass.: Harvard University Press), pp. 33-35. Copyright, 1941, by the President and Fellows of Harvard College.

The true boundary line of the First Amendment can be fixed only when Congress and the courts realize that the principle on which speech is classified as lawful or unlawful involves the balancing against each other of two very important *social* [italics mine] interests, in public safety and in the search for truth. Every reasonable attempt should be made to maintain both interests unimpaired, and the great interest in free speech should be sacrificed only when the interest in public safety is really imperiled, and not, as most men believe, when it is barely conceivable that it may be slightly affected.

Alexander Meiklejohn, in his 1948 treatise on Free Speech: And Its Relation to Self-Government (reprinted in 1960 as part of Political Freedom) concurred with Professor Chafee's distinction between a private and a public interest in speech. He could not, however, accept Chafee's notion that the public interest in free speech could ever be subordinated to any other alleged need, such as that of public safety. While agreeing that the interest in private speech might justifiably be limited by conflicting claims, he felt that the First Amendment was intended, as written, absolutely to forbid abridgment of "the freedom of speech." Therefore he developed a rationale by which this paradox could be resolved. He contended that the freedom of speech spoken of in the First Amendment was meant to apply only to discussion of matters of public policy, and that it was only this kind of speech that might never be abridged. The private right of an individual to express himself on matters unrelated to the business of self-government is, in Meiklejohn's view, protected by the "life, liberty, or property" clause of the Fifth Amendment, which allows for interference if effectuated by "due process of law." By placing the private interest in speech, which it would seem necessary on occasion to abridge, under the same protective cover as the public interest, the latter, Meiklejohn feels, is inevitably watered down.

Alexander Meiklejohn:[2]

. . . the absoluteness of the First Amendment rests
upon the fact that it is not double-minded in reference. It is
single-minded. It has no concern about the "needs of many
men to express their opinions." It provides, not for many
men, but for all men. . . . the First Amendment . . . is
not saying that any man may talk whenever and wherever
he chooses. It is not dealing with that private issue. It is
saying that, as interests, the integrity of public discussion
and the care for the public safety are identical. . . . Shall
we give a hearing to those who hate and despise freedom,
to those who, if they had the power, would destroy our
institutions? Certainly, yes! Our action must be guided, not
by their principles, but by ours. We listen, not because
they desire to speak, but because we need to hear. . . .
When men decide to be self-governed, to take control of
their behavior, the search for truth is not merely one of a
number of interests which may be "balanced," on equal
terms, against one another. In that enterprise, the attempt
to know and to understand has a unique status, a unique
authority, to which all other activities are subordinated. . . .

And it is that authority of these truth-seeking activities
which the First Amendment recognizes as uniquely significant when it says that the freedom of public discussion
shall never be abridged.

The difficulties of the paradox of freedom as applied to
speech may perhaps be lessened if we now examine the
procedure of the traditional American town meeting. . . .
The basic principle is that the freedom of speech shall be
unabridged. And yet the meeting cannot even be opened
unless, by common consent, speech is abridged. A chairman
or moderator is, or has been, chosen. He "calls the meeting
to order." . . . restrictions upon speech have been set up.
. . . certain rules of order will be observed. . . . debaters

---

[2] Reprinted by permission of Harper & Row, Publishers, Inc., from
Alexander Meiklejohn, *Political Freedom*, pp. 55-60, 24-28. Copyright
© 1948, 1960 by Harper & Brothers.

must confine their remarks to "the question before the house." If one man "has the floor," no one else may interrupt him except as provided by the rules. . . . It is not a Hyde Park. It is a parliament or congress. . . . It is not a dialectical free-for-all. It is self-government.

These speech-abridging activities of the town meeting indicate what the First Amendment to the Constitution does not forbid. When self-governing men demand freedom of speech they are not saying that every individual has an unalienable right to speak whenever, wherever, however, he chooses. . . . The common sense of any reasonable society would deny the existence of that unqualified right. No one, for example, may, without consent of nurse or doctor, rise up in a sickroom to argue for his principles or his candidate. In the sickroom, that question is not "before the house." The discussion is, therefore, "out of order." . . .

What, then, does the First Amendment forbid? Here again the town meeting suggests an answer. . . . the point of ultimate interest is not the words of the speakers, but the minds of the hearers. The final aim of the meeting is the voting of wise decisions. The voters, therefore, must be made as wise as possible. The welfare of the community requires that those who decide issues shall understand them. They must know what they are voting about. And this, in turn, requires that so far as time allows, all facts and interests relevant to the problem shall be fully and fairly presented to the meeting. Both facts and interests must be given in such a way that all the alternative lines of action can be wisely measured in relation to one another. . . . That is why freedom of discussion for those minds may not be abridged.

The First Amendment, then, is not the guardian of unregulated talkativeness. . . . If, for example, at a town meeting, twenty like-minded citizens have become a "party," and if one of them has read to the meeting an argument which they have all approved, it would be ludicrously out of order for each of the others to insist on reading it again. No competent moderator would tolerate that wasting of time available for free discussion. What is essential is not that everyone shall speak, but that everything worth saying shall be said. . . . this means that though citizens may, on other grounds, be barred from speaking, they may not be barred because their views are thought to be false or dangerous. No plan of action shall be outlawed because someone in control thinks it unwise, unfair, un-American. . . . When men govern themselves, it is they —and no one else—who must pass judgment upon unwisdom and unfairness and danger. . . . Just so far as, at any point, the citizens who are to decide an issue are denied acquaintance with information or opinion or doubt or disbelief or criticism which is relevant to that issue, just so far the result must be ill-considered, ill-balanced planning for the general good. *It is that mutilation of the thinking process of the community against which the First Amendment to the Constitution is directed.* The principle of the freedom of speech springs from the necessities of the program of self-government. . . .

If, then, on any occasion in the United States it is allowable to say that the Constitution is a good document it is equally allowable, in that situation, to say that the Constitution is a bad document. If a public building may be used in which to say, in time of war, that the war is justified, then the same building may be used in which to say that it is not justified. . . . These conflicting views may be expressed, must be expressed, not because they are valid, but because they are relevant.

But Meiklejohn's view did not go unchallenged by his former student.

Zechariah Chafee, Jr.:[3]

At Brown, Mr. Meiklejohn loved to open his logic class by asking: "If I should tell you that I just saw a unicorn running across the campus, how could you prove that I was wrong?" What he has just seen in the First Amendment is a beautiful unicorn.

---

[3] Reprinted by permission of the publishers from Zechariah Chafee, Jr.'s book review of Alexander Meiklejohn, *Free Speech: And Its Relation to Self-Government,* 62 *Harvard Law Review* 891 (1949), pp. 891 ff. Copyright 1949 by the Harvard Law Review Association.

Is there any historical evidence that the framers of the First Amendment conceived of two freedoms of speech or intended the Amendment to apply only to discussions of matters connected with the process of self-government? Surely they did not link the Amendment with "universal suffrage" as the author insists, because the much-restricted state franchises of 1791 were left completely untouched by the Constitution. . . . Milton's *Areopagitica* advocated freedom for much else besides political tracts. The First Amendment brackets freedom of speech with freedom of press, which Mr. Meiklejohn never mentions. . . . Jefferson's vigorous support of the Philadelphia bookseller, Dufief, when Dufief was arrested for selling a French book on the creation of the world, shows how closely Jefferson connected freedom of the press with freedom of religion and of all thinking. . . .

Moreover, the framers would hardly have relegated science, art, drama, and poetry to the obscure shelter of the Fifth Amendment. . . .

Mr. Meiklejohn's argument that all the freedoms within the First Amendment are not open to any governmental restrictions leans far too heavily on the absolute nature of its language. Even "the free exercise" of religion has been held not to include polygamy or the exhibition of poisonous snakes in church. Especially significant is the contemporaneous evidence that the phrase "freedom of press" was viewed against a background of familiar legal limitations which men of 1791 did not regard as objectionable, such as damage suits for libel. . . .

The truth is, I think, that the framers had no very clear idea as to what they meant by "the freedom of speech or of the press," but we can say three things with reasonable assurance. First, these politicians, lawyers, scholars, churchgoers and *philosophes*, scientists, agriculturalists, and wide readers used the phrase to embrace the whole realm of thought. Second, they intended the First Amendment to give all the protection they desired, and had no idea of supplementing it by the Fifth Amendment. Finally, the freedom which Congress was forbidden to abridge was not, for them, some absolute concept which had never existed on earth. It was the freedom which they believed they already had—what they had wanted before the Revolution and had acquired through independence. In thinking about it, they took for granted the limitations which had been customarily applied in the day-to-day work of the colonial courts.

. . . The most serious weakness in Mr. Meiklejohn's argument is that it rests on his supposed boundary between public speech and private speech. That line is extremely blurred. Take the novel *Strange Fruit,* which was lately suppressed in Massachusetts. It did not discuss any question then before the voters, but it dealt thoughtfully with many problems of the relations between whites and Negroes, a matter of great national concern. Was this under the First Amendment or the Fifth? Birth control is the most personal of matters and yet any discussion of it raises questions of the desirable size of our population, the intelligent rearing of children, dependency, immorality, and clerical control of votes. The truth is that there are public aspects to practically every subject. The satisfactory operation of self-government requires the individual to develop fairness, sympathy, and understanding of other men, a comprehension of economic forces, and some basic purpose in life. He can get help from poems and plays and novels. No matter if Shakespeare and Whitehead do seem very far away from the issues of the next election. . . . This attitude, however, offers such a wide area for the First Amendment that very little is left for his private speech under the Fifth Amendment. For example, if books and plays are public speech, how can they be penalized for gross obscenity or libels?

On the other hand, if private speech does include scholarship and also art and literature, it is shocking to deprive these vital matters of the protection of the inspiring words of the First Amendment.

We have seen on many occasions earlier in this volume that the U. S. Supreme Court shares Professor Chafee's view rather than Professor Meiklejohn's on the question of the absoluteness of the First Amendment. That the Court

*also follows Chafee rather than Meiklejohn on the private
v. public speech issue is evident from its handling of the
Winters case, in which the argument had been presented
to the Court that allegedly salacious literature should not
be protected by the First Amendment because it contains
no ideas.*

WINTERS v. NEW YORK [4]

Mr. Justice Reed delivered the opinion of the Court.

. . . We do not accede to appellee's suggestion that
the constitutional protection for a free press applies only to
the exposition of ideas. The line between the informing
and the entertaining is too elusive for the protection of that
basic right. Everyone is familiar with instances of propaganda through fiction. What is one man's amusement,
teaches another's doctrine. Though we can see nothing of
any possible value to society in these magazines, they are as
much entitled to the protection of free speech as the best
of literature. . . .

*The Supreme Court's assumption here that propaganda
and artistic expression cannot be divorced, and that the
latter serves a public purpose, receives weighty support
from the testimony of one of our greatest artists of the
spoken word.*

George Bernard Shaw:[5]

I am a specialist in immoral and heretical plays. My reputation has been gained by my persistent struggle to force
the public to reconsider its morals. In particular, I regard
much current morality as to economic and sexual relations
as disastrously wrong; and I regard certain doctrines of the
Christian religion as understood in England to-day with
abhorrence. I write plays with the deliberate object of con-

---

[4] 333 US 507 (1948).
[5] Reprinted by permission of the Public Trustee and The Society of
Authors from George Bernard Shaw, "Preface on the Censorship," in
The Shewing-Up of Blanco Posnet (New York: Brentano's, 1913), pp.
28-29.

verting the nation to my opinions in these matters. . . . I object to censorship not merely because the existing form of it grievously injures and hinders me individually, but on public grounds.

. . . Now morality is extremely valuable to society. It imposes conventional conduct on the great mass of persons who are incapable of original ethical judgment, and who would be quite lost if they were not in leading-strings devised by lawgivers, philosophers, prophets and poets for their guidance. But morality is not dependent on censorship for protection. It is already powerfully fortified by the magistracy and the whole body of law. Blasphemy, indecency, libel, treason, sedition, obscenity, profanity, and all the other evils which a censorship is supposed to avert, are punishable by the civil magistrate with all the severity of vehement prejudice. Morality has not only every engine that lawgivers can devise in full operation for its protection, but also that enormous weight of public opinion enforced by social ostracism which is stronger than all the statutes. A censor pretending to protect morality is like a child pushing the cushions of a railway carriage to give itself the sensation of making the train travel at sixty miles an hour. It is immorality, not morality, that needs protection; it is morality, not immorality, that needs restraint; for morality, with all the dead weight of human inertia and superstition to hang on the back of the pioneer, and all the malice of vulgarity and prejudice to threaten him, is responsible for many persecutions and many martyrdoms.

Persecutions and martyrdoms, however, are trifles compared to the mischief done by censorships in delaying the general march of enlightenment.

. . . It is no more possible for me to do my work honestly as a playwright without giving pain than it is for a dentist. The nation's morals are like its teeth: the more decayed they are the more it hurts to touch them. Prevent dentists and dramatists from giving pain, and not only will our morals become as carious as our teeth, but toothache and the plagues that follow neglected morality will presently cause more agony than all the dentists and dramatists at their worst have caused since the world began.

Although few, if any, scholars today would dispute the proposition that Shaw's plays merit the protection of freedom of speech, there are some who would still argue for certain kinds of distinctions based upon the social value of a communication.

John E. Coons: [6]

Few of us would brook interference with mere expression in the areas of politics, religion, or science under any circumstances, but is it politically unprincipled to feel less concern about advertising, invective, and erotica? Is a constitutional hierarchy of subject matter and its graduated freedoms of speech utterly indefensible? . . . One could conceivably argue that, instead of preserving free expression, a unitary freedom of all types of speech—a freedom limited only by the clear and present danger standard— really endangers and erodes areas of important ideas by coupling them with areas of speech involving less crucial consequences for a free society. By treating advertising on a par with politics we may degrade politics to the extent that we hallow the huckster.

This view received aid and comfort from the U. S. Supreme Court in Roth when "redeeming social importance" was introduced as a measure of a publication's permissibility. It would appear, therefore, that we are left with some inconsistency yet to be clarified between the Roth and Winters opinions.

Another confusion charged against the Court is that it has failed, in its allegedly inconsistent and wide-ranging application of the clear-and-present-danger test, to make distinctions which some critics feel should be made between cases involving political heresy and those in the other areas of communication we have discussed in Chapters 1 and 3.

---

[6] Reprinted by special permission of Northwestern University School of Law from John E. Coons' book review of Richard McKeon, Robert K. Merton, and Walter Gellhorn, *The Freedom to Read,* 53 *Northwestern University Law Review* 127 (1958), p. 129. Copyright © 1958 by Northwestern University School of Law.

Walter Berns:[7]

In order to avoid the terms of the First Amendment
while simultaneously jailing those who threatened the security of the nation, the 1919 Court devised the clear and
present danger test. The modern, more libertarian justices
have converted this into an absolute principle to be used
not only in national security cases but in all First Amendment cases coming before the Court. All speech that falls
short of threatening the security of the nation is to go un-
punished, which results in a definition of justice not as
everyone getting what he deserves but as the maximum
amount of personal freedom compatible with national security. But whether a judicial scale that weighs only freedom defined as license, on the one hand, and national
security, on the other, is the correct measurement of these
speech cases, is a question whose gravity cannot be dismissed by anyone interested in the defense of what men of
another era called virtue.

Used in cases as remote from the situation in the Schenck
case as those involving labor picketing and contempt of
court, it is no wonder that the clear and present danger test
was almost unrecognizable by the time the Court called
upon it to convict Dennis. But despite Professor Fellman's
sardonic remark, "Whether the clear and present danger
doctrine will survive much longer under the crushing weight
of the Chief Justice's loving devotion remains to be seen,"
it was not Vinson's fault that the test was not the chaste,
unsullied debutante of 1919; it had spent over thirty years
in the streets.

*To Berns, the Supreme Court has been guilty of failing
to protect the nation's virtue by allowing the same broad
freedom to artistic expression and intergroup contention as
to political discussion. But to another critic the Court's
fault is that it has been too willing to use different tests for*

---

[7] Reprinted by permission of the publishers from Walter Berns, *Freedom, Virtue and the First Amendment*, pp. 71-72, 56. Copyright ©
1957 by the Louisiana State University Press.

different kinds of speech. To him the Roth decision's establishment of two categories of communication calling for separate but unequal treatment was a serious error.

Harry Kalven, Jr.:[8]

Mr. Justice Brennan [in Roth] turned to meet the challenge that there must be a clear and present danger of something to justify regulation of speech. He is thus on the very threshold of the perplexities which so entranced Judge Frank. He disposed of them with one quick thrust: since obscenity is not in the area of constitutionally protected speech, it is, quoting Beauharnais v. Illinois, "unnecessary either for us or for the state courts to consider the issues behind the phrase 'clear and present danger.' " The Court thus found further use for the two-level free-speech theory which made its first appearance in Chaplinsky and was given status as doctrine in Beauharnais. The spectacular dilemma predicted for the Court when it confronted the perplexities of obscenity regulation turned out to have no horns at all. The perplexities may be puzzling but, the Court said, they are simply not relevant.

After putting obscenity so securely beyond the pale of constitutional concern, Mr. Justice Brennan hastened to add a good word on behalf of sex: "Sex and obscenity are not synonymous." Then followed what must be the least controversial utterance in the Court's history: "Sex, a great and mysterious motive force in human life, has indisputably been a subject of absorbing interest to mankind through the ages." But obscene discussions of sex are not entitled to the protection afforded fundamental freedoms. . . .

The two-level speech theory, although it afforded the Court a statesmanlike way around a dilemma, seems difficult to accept as doctrine. It is perhaps understandable in the context of Chaplinsky, where the speech in question is

---

[8] Reprinted by permission of the publishers from Harry Kalven, Jr., "The Metaphysics of the Law of Obscenity," in Philip B. Kurland, ed., The Supreme Court Review, 1960, pp. 9-16. Copyright © 1960 by The University of Chicago Press.

nothing more complex than the utterance of "son of a bitch," said rapidly. In connection with libel, as in *Beauharnais*, or obscenity, as in *Roth*, however, it seems a strained effort to trap a problem. At one level there are communications which, even though odious to the majority opinion of the day, even though expressive of the thought we hate, are entitled to be measured against the clear-and-present danger criterion. At another level are communications apparently so worthless as not to require any extensive judicial effort to determine whether they can be prohibited. There is to be freedom for the thought we hate, but not for the candor we deplore. The doctrinal apparatus is thus quite intricate. In determining the constitutionality of any ban on a communication, the first question is whether it belongs to a category that has any social utility. If it does not, it may be banned. If it does, there is a further question of measuring the clarity and proximity and gravity of any danger from it. It is thus apparent that the issue of social utility of a communication has become as crucial a part of our theory as the issue of its danger. Although the Court has not yet made this clear it must be assumed that the Court's concern is with the utility of a category of communication rather than with a particular instance. . . . everything now depends on what is meant by obscene. If the Court's formula is to make any sense, it must place a heavy burden on the definition of obscenity. . . .

It has long been clear that certain classics—Aristophanes, Rabelais, Boccaccio, Shakespeare, Montaigne, Voltaire, Balzac, and, some would add, the Bible itself—have been immune from obscenity regulation. . . . The abortive effort of the Postmaster a few years back to bar *Lysistrata* was greeted with, and defeated by, laughter. . . . On the two-level theory, the classics do not need a special privilege; they fall automatically into speech on the first level, and hence automatically outside the realm of the constitutionally obscene. To put this another way, the Court is giving constitutional privilege to all communication that has some social value. And Judge Frank's pointed query as to why obscenity embedded in a classic was less dangerous than obscenity in a book without literary distinction is not so pointed now, since the latter is banned not because it is dangerous but because it is worthless. . . . it is unclear how the formula will help a future Court faced with the question whether a particular item can be banned constitutionally. . . . The classic defense of John Stuart Mill and the modern defense of Alexander Meiklejohn do not help much when the question is why the novel, the poem, the painting, the drama, or the piece of sculpture falls within the protection of the First Amendment. Nor do the famous opinions of Hand, Holmes, and Brandeis. The emphasis is all on truth winning out in a fair fight between competing ideas. The emphasis is clearest in Meiklejohn's argument that free speech is indispensable to the informed citizenry required to make democratic self-government work. The people need free speech because they vote. . . . Not all communications are relevant to the political process. The people do not need novels or dramas or paintings or poems because they will be called upon to vote. Art and belles-lettres do not deal in such ideas—at least not good art or belles-lettres—and it makes little sense here to talk, as Mr. Justice Brandeis did in his great opinion in *Whitney*, of whether there is still time for counter-speech. Thus there seems to be a hiatus in our basic free-speech theory.

If Professor Kalven is right, that a hiatus exists in our theory, we had best reconcile ourselves to continued controversy in this area until a more satisfactory rationale is evolved. But whether we ultimately settle on a two-level, three-level, or unitary definition of speech we will still not escape the problem of what to do when speech, however defined, comes into conflict with other valid and constitutionally protected interests. We have already seen this question arise with regard to the nation's desire to raise an army, or a community's wish to protect the repose of its citizens from loud-speakers. But there are other knotty problems as well. At what point does freedom of speech or press impair an individual's right to a fair trial? What about the unsolicited mailing of pornographic pictures to youngsters? And perhaps the most difficult of all, to what degree may free speech be permitted to interfere with another man's right to privacy? A recent volume by Morris L. Ernst and Alan U. Schwartz, Privacy: The Right to be Let Alone, deals extensively with this issue. Professor Chafee provides us with an interesting example of the problem.

Zechariah Chafee, Jr.:[9]

. . . *Lovell* v. *Griffin* and its successors make it rather difficult for a city to frame an ordinance to keep its streets clean from communicative papers. Perhaps this does not greatly matter. Handbills are almost the only available way for poor men to express ideas to the public or announce a protest meeting. The talk about dirty streets and sidewalks often looks like just a pretense for suppressing unpopular causes. . . .

House to house canvassing raises more serious problems. Of all the methods of spreading unpopular ideas, this seems the least entitled to extensive protection. The possibilities of persuasion are slight compared with the certainties of annoyance. . . . home is one place where a man ought to be able to shut himself up in his own ideas if he desires. There he should be free not only from unreasonable searches and seizures, but also from hearing uninvited strangers expound distasteful doctrines. A doorbell cannot be disregarded like a handbill. It takes several minutes to ascertain the purpose of a propagandist and at least several more to get rid of him. . . . A housewife may fairly claim some protection from being obliged to leave off bathing the baby and rush down to the door. . . . Freedom of the home is as important as freedom of speech. I cannot help wondering whether the Justices of the Supreme Court are quite aware of the effect of organized front-door intrusions upon people who are not sheltered from zealots and imposters by a staff of servants or the locked entrance of an apartment house.

---

[9] Reprinted by permission of the publishers from Zechariah Chafee, Jr., *Free Speech in the United States* (Cambridge, Mass.: Harvard University Press), pp. 406-07. Copyright, 1941, by the President and Fellows of Harvard College.

But whenever we begin weighing other interests against speech, as inevitably we must, there always looms the danger that this precious first freedom may be rationalized away. This is the very peril which Justice Hugo Black sees in the increasing use by our courts of the so-called "balancing doctrine." He spoke to this issue at length when a majority of his colleagues upheld a decision of the California courts which allowed that state to deny admission to the bar to Raphael Konigsberg because he refused to answer questions relating to his membership in the Communist Party. Konigsberg did affirm his disbelief in violent overthrow of government and stated that he was never knowingly a member of any organization which advocated such action. The majority opinion admitted that a man's speech and associations might be deterred by the knowledge that subsequent disclosure could be forced from him, but felt that the state's interest outweighed this consideration.

KONIGSBERG v. STATE BAR OF CALIFORNIA[10]

Mr. Justice Black, with whom the Chief Justice and Mr. Justice Douglas concur, dissenting.

. . . The recognition that California has subjected "speech and association to the deterrence of subsequent disclosure" is, under the First Amendment, sufficient in itself to render the action of the State unconstitutional unless one subscribes to the doctrine that permits constitutionally protected rights to be "balanced" away whenever a majority of this Court thinks that a State might have interest sufficient to justify abridgment of those freedoms. As I have indicated many times before, I do not subscribe to that doctrine for I believe that the First Amendment's unequivocal command that there shall be no abridgment of the rights of free speech and assembly shows that the men who drafted our Bill of Rights did all the "balancing" that was to be done in this field. The history of the First Amendment is too well known to require repeating here except to say that it certainly cannot be denied that the very object of adopting the First Amendment, as well as

---

[10] 366 US 36 (1961).

the other provisions of the Bill of Rights, was to put the freedoms protected there completely out of the area of any congressional control that may be attempted through the exercise of precisely those powers that are now being used to "balance" the Bill of Rights out of existence. . . .

The Court attempts to justify its refusal to apply the plain mandate of the First Amendment in part by reference to the so-called "clear and present danger test" forcefully used by Mr. Justice Holmes and Mr. Justice Brandeis, not to narrow but to broaden the then prevailing interpretation of First Amendment freedoms. I think very little can be found in anything they ever said that would provide support for the "balancing test" presently in use. Indeed, the idea of "balancing" away First Amendment freedoms appears to me to be wholly inconsistent with the view, strongly espoused by Justices Holmes and Brandeis, that the best test of truth is the power of the thought to get itself accepted in the competition of the market. The "clear and present danger test" was urged as consistent with this view in that it protected speech in all cases except those in which danger was so imminent that there was no time for rational discussion. The "balancing test," on the other hand, rests upon the notion that some ideas are so dangerous that the government need not restrict itself to contrary arguments as a means of opposing them even where there is ample time to do so. Thus here, where there is not a semblance of a "clear and present danger" and where there is more than ample time in which to combat by discussion any idea which may be involved, the majority permits the State of California to adopt measures calculated to suppress the advocacy of views about governmental affairs.

I recognize, of course, that the "clear and present danger test," though itself a great advance toward individual liberty over some previous notions of the protections afforded by the First Amendment, does not go as far as my own views as to the protection that should be accorded these freedoms. I agree with Justices Holmes and Brandeis, however, that the primary purpose of the First Amendment was to insure that all ideas would be allowed to enter the "competition of the market." But I fear that the creation of "tests" by which speech is left unprotected under certain circumstances is a standing invitation to abridge it. This is nowhere more clearly indicated than by the sudden transformation of the "clear and present danger test" in *Dennis* v. *United States*. In that case, this Court accepted Judge Learned Hand's "restatement" of the "clear and present danger test" . . . there seems to me to be much room to doubt that Justices Holmes and Brandeis would even have recognized their test. . . .

The Court suggests that a "literal reading of the First Amendment" would be totally unreasonable because it would invalidate many widely accepted laws. I do not know to what extent this is true. I do not believe, for example, that it would invalidate laws resting upon the premise that where speech is an integral part of unlawful conduct that is going on at the time, the speech can be used to illustrate, emphasize and establish the unlawful conduct. On the other hand, it certainly would invalidate all laws that abridge the right of the people to discuss matters of religious or public interest, in the broadest meaning of those terms, for it is clear that a desire to protect this right was the primary purpose of the First Amendment. Some people have argued, with much force, that the freedoms guaranteed by the First Amendment are limited to somewhat broad areas like those. But I believe this Nation's security and tranquility can best be served by giving the First Amendment the same broad construction that all Bill of Rights guarantees deserve.

The danger of failing to construe the First Amendment in this manner is, I think, dramatically illustrated by the decision of this Court in *Beauharnais* v. *People of State of Illinois*, one of the cases relied upon for this holding today. In that case, a majority of this Court upheld the conviction of a man whose only "crime" was the circulation of a petition to be presented to the City Council of Chicago urging that body to follow a policy of racial segregation in language that the State of Illinois chose to regard as "libelous" against Negroes. . . . Beauharnais was held to have simultaneously "libelled" some fifteen million people. And by this tremendous expansion of the concept of "libel," what some people might regard as a relatively minor exception to the full protection of freedom of speech had suddenly become a vehicle which could be used to justify a return to the vicious era of the law of seditious libel, in which the political party in power, both in England and in this country, used such laws to put their opponents in jail.

Whatever may be the wisdom, however, of an approach that would reject exceptions to the plain language of the First Amendment based upon such things as "libel," "obscenity" or "fighting words," such is not the issue in this case. For the majority does not, and surely would not, contend that the kind of speech involved in this case—wholly related as it is to conflicting ideas about governmental affairs and policies—falls outside the protection of the First Amendment, however narrowly that Amendment may be interpreted. So the only issue presently before us is whether speech that must be well within the protection of the Amendment should be given complete protection or whether it is entitled only to such protection as is consistent in the minds of a majority of this Court with whatever interest the Government may be asserting to justify its abridgment. The Court, by stating unequivocally that there are no "absolutes" under the First Amendment, necessarily takes the position that even speech that is admittedly protected by the First Amendment is subject to the "balancing test" and that therefore no kind of speech is to be protected if the Government can assert an interest of sufficient weight to induce this Court to uphold its abridgment. In my judgment, such a sweeping denial of the existence of any inalienable right to speak undermines the very foundation upon which the First Amendment, the Bill of Rights, and, indeed, our entire structure of government rests. The Founders of this Nation attempted to set up a limited government which left certain rights in the people—rights that could not be taken away without amendment of the basic charter of government. The majority's "balancing test" tells us that this is not so. It tells us that no right to think, speak or publish exists in the people that cannot be taken away if the Government finds it sufficiently imperative or expedient to do so. Thus, the "balancing test" turns our "Government of the people, by the people and for the people" into a government over the people.

. . . examples also serve to illustrate the difference between the sort of "balancing" that the majority has been doing and the sort of "balancing" that was intended when that concept was first accepted as a method for insuring the complete protection of First Amendment freedoms even against purely incidental or inadvertent consequences. The term came into use chiefly as a result of the cases in which the power of municipalities to keep their streets open for normal traffic was attacked by groups wishing to use those streets for religious or political purposes. . . . we recognized that the enforcement of even these ordinances, which attempted no regulation at all of the content of speech and which were neither openly nor surreptitiously aimed at speech, could bring about an "incidental" abridgment of speech. So we went on to point out that even ordinances directed at and regulating only conduct might be invalidated if, after "weighing" the reasons for regulating the particular conduct, we found them insufficient to justify diminishing "the exercise of rights so vital to the maintenance of democratic institutions" as those of the First Amendment.

But those cases never intimated that we would uphold as constitutional an ordinance which purported to rest upon the power of a city to regulate traffic but which was aimed at speech or attempted to regulate the content of speech.

. . . I realize that there has been considerable talk, even in the opinions of this Court, to the effect that "advocacy" is not "speech." But with the highest respect for those who believe that there is such a distinction, I cannot agree with it. . . .

In my judgment this case must take its place in the ever-lengthening line of cases in which individual liberty to think, speak, write, associate and petition is being abridged in a manner precisely contrary to the explicit commands of the First Amendment. And I believe the abridgment of liberty here, as in most of the other cases in that line, is based upon nothing more than a fear that the American people can be alienated from their allegiance to our form of government by the talk of zealots for a form of government that is hostile to everything for which this country now stands or ever has stood. I think this fear is groundless for I believe that the loyalty and patriotism of the American people toward our own free way of life are too deeply rooted to be shaken by mere talk or argument from people who are wedded to totalitarian forms of government. . . .

QUESTIONS FOR DISCUSSION

1. Can anything be found in the opinions presented in this book by Justice Black that might explain his failure to dissent from the Court's unanimous 1942 decision in Chaplinsky?

2. Meiklejohn would extend the First Amendment only to speech having to do with the process of self-government, but there he would apply it absolutely. Chafee rejects the absolutist position but would have the First Amendment apply to all forms of expression. Which point of view would seem to provide the broadest protection for freedom of speech?

3. What does Kalven mean by the "two-level" theory of freedom of speech?

4. Kalven asserts that "not all communications are relevant to the political process." Might this contention be disputed?

5. Do curbs on the use of loud-speaking equipment or on door-to-door solicitations entail the same kind of "balancing of interests" to which Justice Black objects in Konigsberg?

5

Why Freedom of Speech?
Challenge and Response

———————◆———————

"It is error alone which needs the support of government. Truth can stand by itself."
—Thomas Jefferson,
Notes on Virginia, Query 17

One cannot read the opinions that have been presented thus far without developing a considerable sense of the stakes involved in controversies over freedom of speech. Much has been expressed and even more implied concerning the justifications for restricting or liberating the spoken word. But a great deal has also been taken for granted by writers who assume agreement or understanding where it may not in fact exist regarding the values of freedom or restraint. We cannot properly conclude our exploration of the problems of freedom of speech without reviewing in a more explicit way the philosophical premises which underlie the leading points of view.

The most basic challenge posed to the libertarian position centers around the question of whether freedom itself is an ultimate good or merely a means to more valuable ends. If it is the latter, we are then led to inquire whether there are other means which may sometimes be more appropriate to the achievement of our goals.

There is and always has been a considerable body of philosophic thought that holds that there are, indeed, other ends and other means more valuable than freedom. Among the leading representatives of that position on the current American scene are the orthodox spokesmen of the Roman Catholic Church. Father Harold Gardiner is one of these.

Harold C. Gardiner, S.J.:[1]

Authority arises from the fact of each individual's free will: it is because each one has free will that individuality must be harnessed, so to speak, if the individuals are to pull as a team for the cohesion and advancement of the community. . . .

This is true not merely from a consideration of the origin of society and of the authority which is necessary for the very existence of society, but from a consideration of the purpose or end for which society exists. That end or purpose, in general, is the common good, the good of society as a whole as distinguished from the good of the individuals who make up the whole. . . .

Coercion is never pleasant for those being coerced and, quite obviously, coercion can overstep proper bounds and turn into injustice and tyranny. But coercion that is exercised as a means to prevent the frustration of the common good is worthy of respect and love as is the authority it is designed to uphold. . . . Restrictions are valid only if they are for the sake of a greater good, a greater liberty. . . . not even the restrictions which God's law puts on our human actions are good *merely* because they are restrictions. The negative precepts of the Ten Commandments look always to a positive freedom. . . . clearing away the roadblocks thrown up by our pride and sensuality so that the greater freedom may operate. . . .

If the coercive aspect of law and authority is looked on in this way, as a means toward a greater freedom, the pedagogical aspect of coercion becomes clear. . . . St. Thomas Aquinas has much to say on this. . . . Here, for instance, is one commentary. . . . "By compelling bad boys from doing wrong, a twofold result is secured: first, the tranquil-

---

[1] Reprinted by permission of the publishers from Harold C. Gardiner, S.J., *Catholic Viewpoint on Censorship*, pp. 20-29, 37-43. Copyright © 1958, 1961 by Doubleday & Company, Inc.

lity of honest people is assured; secondly, the bad boys themselves get used to acting honestly, so that they may finally become virtuous, having become able to do voluntarily what they previously did by fear of punishment. . . . a good habit generated by fear, although non-virtuous in its origin, makes virtue easier, the substitution of good will for fear taking place easily when the exterior acts of virtue have become habitual. Coercion, in the long run, paves the way for persuasion, because habitual automatism turns to voluntariness." . . . in this matter of censorship, protests by such organizations as the American Civil Liberties Union against any and all exercises of "censorship" all too often sound as though they are based on the assumption that all coercion exercised by authority is a bad and evil thing. . . . false assumption that whatever, especially in a democracy, curtails freedom (but what *type* of freedom is rarely defined, though here lies the specific problem) impedes "progress." The Catholic concept, on the other hand, holds that the very idea of human progress implies necessarily the correlative idea of measure and restraint. . . .

The suspicion that the coercive aspects of authority and law are not to be tolerated by free men is a holdover from the philosophical liberalism of the nineteenth century. . . . Let truth go out and jostle with error in the market place . . . do not restrain or limit error and the expression of it, and the truth will always win out. Now, certainly the Catholic position entertains the utmost respect for the power of truth . . . and for its ultimate triumph, but that respect is not so naive as to believe that here and now, in these circumstances, when the truth should already have won and its delayed victory imperils the common good, error must be left uncontrolled. . . . philosophical liberalism is the rather naive idolatry of the power of mere education, and by that is meant any educative process that insists exclusively on the freedom to examine and learn. . . . This stand is based . . . on the prior assumption that the truth will always vanquish error if allowed to compete on an equal footing. But any "equal footing" rests on the further assumption that all men are equal in taste, inclination to virtue, powers of self-control. . . . even the foes of all and every censorship are themselves constrained to admit, that some people who have indeed been exposed to "good" literature throughout many years of education still seem to prefer the "art" and "girlie" magazines. . . .

This is not to underestimate the power of education but simply to restate that the educative process, no less than the process of law, necessarily entails a restrictive or coercive element. If the goal of education is a glorious and positive "do"—*do* grow into the full stature of integral manhood—it can be reached only by some inculcation of many a "don't." . . . "Without the aid of *trained* . . . emotions, the intellect is powerless against the animal organism." . . .

It follows . . . that society, which has the right and duty to establish laws for the common good, has, by the same title, the right *and the duty* to exercise coercion. . . . A great number of those who oppose censorship in any shape or form deny implicitly (though they may never advert to the fact) that society has the *right* to censor. . . . We aver in these pages that the state not only has the *right* but is solemnly bound by the *duty* to censor, under certain circumstances.

. . . The fundamental "oughtness" under which a man can alone act with full freedom is not an "oughtness" that is merely handed down by wise men, by courts or judges or counselors. It is an "oughtness" that is handed to man by the faculty of his reason. This is not merely Catholic doctrine; it is a datum of common sense and experience. If a man *knows* that the world is shaped something like a Florida orange, is he free to say that he knows it is as flat as an Aunt Jemima pancake? Why, yes; he is free, if he wants to use his free will in that fantastic fashion. But if he so uses his free will—not merely in joke, but in consistent fashion —would not common sense say that he is a slave to prejudice, whim, a warped sense of humor, a perverted desire to be different? In the face of a recognized fact, there is no intellectual freedom to deny that fact. But this is not slavery; it is freedom in truth. . . .

Again I quote Maritain. . . . "The 'objective order that is imposed on man' is, in a general way, that of the nature of things with their respective laws (and first and foremost human nature) and the order of truth and of supernatural life: it flows from the Eternal Law which is the Wisdom of the Maker of all things. . . ."

There is a sense in which we can legitimately say that this "objective order of things" is imposed on human action, not indeed by those who are "competent" simply because they have power, but by those who have power because they are "competent." . . .

But—and here is the crucial point—this imposition is not arbitrary. . . . it is a statement of what is *reasonable* for a man to do, not only with respect to his private life, but primarily with respect to the life of the community. . . . *Is* there, many ask, any objective order in moral acts? Who can define precisely what is right, what wrong? . . . This is to confuse the issue. The point is not whether the judges (the censors) are themselves law-abiding, good, or prudent; the point is whether there are objective reasons for the law and whether the judges know and apply these reasons. . . . the reasonableness, the authority, the majesty of the civil law do not depend on any personal qualities of law-giver or law-enforcer. . . . we "salute the uniform, not the man."

Freedom adequately defined, then, is, in the Catholic view, only "freedom to act as I ought." And the oughtness comes not from any quality of goodness or wisdom in those who "tell" me what I ought to do but from the reasonableness of the law, which can be *applied* only by the judges— not "cooked up" by them and "imposed."

The argument of the Catholic Church, at least as represented here by Father Gardiner, might be summarized by the following propositions:

    1. *The ultimate goal of man is the "common good."*

    2. *There exists a body of "natural law" that defines the common good.*

    3. *These laws are clear to educated and reasonable men, but since all men do not always freely choose to fol-*

low them, authority must be established to enforce them.

4. True freedom is the freedom to do only what one ought (i.e., in conformity with natural law as defined by competent authority) rather than to do whatever one's desires may dictate.

Another author, whose views seem compatible with these propositions, elaborates the anti-libertarian position.

Walter Berns:[2]

Despite the extensive use made of the *Areopagitica* to buttress modern arguments for freedom, in it Milton was arguing only against prior censorship of the press; he said nothing directly about speech. This distinction may be of no significance in the modern western world, where practically every adult is able to read, but during the seventeenth century the difference between the number of Englishmen who could read and those who could only speak and listen was tremendous. Perhaps the difference corresponded roughly to those who could be trusted to choose truth when it grappled with falsehood and those who could not be so trusted.

. . . The decisive difference between Milton and those modern libertarians who decorate their pages with excerpts culled from the *Areopagitica* is that Milton believed in virtue and the necessity of it in society. He wrote under no illusions that the differences between the moral and the immoral, the good and the evil, were merely matters of taste, and of no political significance. In fact, the only legitimate service Milton's *Areopagitica* can be made to perform for the libertarians is to point up the practical aspects of the problem of censorship. No one has done this as powerfully as he has; but even the most powerful argument of this sort is not, however perplexing the problem of getting intelligent and perceptive censors, an argument against the need for censorship. . . .

[2] Reprinted by permission of the publishers from Walter Berns, *Freedom, Virtue and the First Amendment*, pp. 23, 125-28, 164-65. Copyright © 1957 by the Louisiana State University Press.

Milton recognizes the place of virtue and the legitimate interest of the government in the virtue of its citizens. . . . In his essay on education . . . he leaves no doubt that children are to be subjected to a rigorous educational discipline, which continues until the child becomes an adult over twenty years of age: there is to be no freedom for children to choose. "Then will be required a special reinforcement of constant and sound endoctrinating to set them right and firm, instructing them more amply in the knowledge of Vertue and the hatred of Vice. . . ." . . . Educated men are to be free to choose; and, may we fairly add, *only* educated men.

. . . is the good life merely the free life? Is it merely a life in which a man is permitted to speak, publish, and worship in his own way, without guidance from moral principle or guidance by the law in the name of moral principle? And can the differences between political regimes, especially the decisive differences, be rendered in terms of the amount of personal freedom enjoyed by their citizens, or by the amount of power and scope of authority exercised by their governors? Is not something of overwhelming importance concealed by describing both the Nazi regime and the regime of Salazar in Portugal, or for that matter the Fascist regime of Mussolini, with the one term totalitarian? What is in fact concealed is the monstrous evil of the Nazi regime.

The plain fact is that not all free speech is good speech. Which means that freedom of speech is not always a sound or just public policy. . . .

There is always the danger that the abridgment of vicious speech will be followed by the abridgment of good, or virtuous speech, but the Court would be in a position to permit the former and prohibit the latter if it developed principles that recognize the difference between vice and virtue. Supreme Court opinions may deny that such distinctions may properly be made by any official of a democratic government, but this is to deny what the Court is doing all the time—even when it fails to act—when it separates the legal from the illegal. Whether bad speech is denominated "fighting words," obscenity, or incitations to breaches of the peace, it constitutes an authoritative definition of what is not to be permitted. . . .

The Court's dilemma has been that it is provided with a constitutional provision and a body of thought which say, or appear to say, that freedom shall not be and ought not to be abridged because freedom is good, but provided also with sufficient common sense to know that it must be abridged sometimes, as the cases show, because it is not necessarily good. It has lacked, however, a wise principle to guide its decisions and is fearful of establishing a precedent of abridgment. . . .

The law of the First Amendment is in a condition of confusion, and no member of the Court can be absolved of all blame for this confusion. Judicial principles have been misapplied to achieve results which cannot serve as precedents. The basic reason for this has been the attempt to identify freedom as the hallmark of life under the American government, or as the greatest of all goods, the good to be protected and fostered above all others. Thus, the justices refuse to distinguish between the inherent worth of the ideas expressed, which, concededly, is a practice fraught with danger. Nevertheless, they are inevitably forced to make the choice on these grounds, though they may disguise what they are doing; the only escape from this choice is to insist that nothing is superior to freedom. However often this is asserted from the bench, no justice has carried out this proposition in practice.

What Berns is claiming here is that the U. S. Supreme Court does in fact assume the authoritative role of making moral choices between good and bad speech, but disguises them as legal judgments of constitutionality. Rather than urging the Court to abdicate this function entirely, as the libertarian might, he asks that they perform it more frankly, more rigorously, and more consistently.

That Berns places lower priority on individual freedom and the democratic process than on the maintenance of other moral values he believes important is made clear when he declares that the primary evil of a dictatorship is not its form of government but the particular goals to which it subscribes. He thus rejects the basic premise of libertarianism, to which we now turn, which holds that only in an open society can we be confident that the most desirable values, beyond freedom itself, will prevail. Libertarians may or may not believe in the existence of "absolute good," but they are united in their skepticism toward anyone who claims the ability to define it absolutely, particularly for others than himself.

———————◆———————

The arguments on behalf of free speech have been summarized by one scholar in four points.

Thomas I. Emerson:[3]

A. *Individual Self-Fulfillment*

The right to freedom of expression is justified first of all as the right of an individual purely in his capacity as an individual. It derives from the widely accepted premise of Western thought that the proper end of man is the realization of his character and potentialities as a human being. . . . thought and communication are the fountainhead of all expression of the individual personality. To cut off the flow at the source is to dry up the whole stream. . . .

B. *Attainment of Truth*

. . . suppression of information, discussion, or the clash of opinion prevents one from reaching the most rational judgment, blocks the generation of new ideas, and tends to perpetuate error. . . .

C. *Participation in Decision-Making*

. . . Once one accepts the premise of the Declaration of Independence—that governments derive "their just powers from the consent of the governed"—it follows that the governed must, in order to exercise their right of consent, have full freedom of expression. . . .

---

[3] Reprinted by permission of the copyright holder from the *Yale Law Journal*, Volume 72, Number 5, p. 16. Copyright © 1963 by Yale Law Journal Co., Inc.

D. *Balance Between Stability and Change*

. . . open discussion is a method . . . of maintaining the precarious balance between healthy cleavage and necessary consensus. . . . coercion of expression is likely to be ineffective. While it may prevent social change, at least for a time, it cannot eradicate thought or belief; nor can it promote loyalty or unity. . . .

Again, suppression of expression conceals the real problems confronting a society and diverts public attention from the critical issues. It is likely to result in neglect of the grievances which are the actual basis of the unrest, and thus prevent their correction. . . . society is more likely to be subject to general inertia than to volatile change. Hence resistance to the political order is unlikely to reach the stage of disorder unless a substantial section of the population is living under seriously adverse or discriminatory conditions. Only a government which consistently fails to relieve valid grievances need fear the outbreak of violent opposition. Thus, given the inertia which so often characterizes a society, freedom of expression, far from causing upheaval, is more properly viewed as a leavening process, facilitating necessary social and political change and keeping a society from stultification and decay.

The most extensive and incisive statement of the rationale for freedom of expression, unsurpassed by any other, remains that written by John Stuart Mill in 1858. To Mill the case against suppression of opinion was three-fold.

> 1. *The suppressed opinion may be true, and the accepted beliefs in error.*
> 2. *Even if true, accepted beliefs become mere prejudices if unchallenged and untested.*
> 3. *There is likely to be some basis for all opinions.*

John Stuart Mill:[4]

. . . If all mankind minus one, were of one opinion, and only one person were of the contrary opinion, mankind

---

[4] From John Stuart Mill, "On Liberty," in Charles W. Eliot, ed., *The Harvard Classics* (P. F. Collier & Son, 1909), pp. 219-52.

would be no more justified in silencing that one person, than he, if he had the power, would be justified in silencing mankind. Were an opinion a personal possession of no value except to the owner; if to be obstructed in the enjoyment of it were simply a private injury, it would make some difference whether the injury was inflicted only on a few persons or on many. But the peculiar evil of silencing the expression of an opinion is, that it is robbing the human race; posterity as well as the existing generation; those who dissent from the opinion, still more than those who hold it. If the opinion is right, they are deprived of the opportunity of exchanging error for truth: if wrong, they lose, what is almost as great a benefit, the clearer perception and livelier impression of truth, produced by its collision with error. . . .

First: the opinion which it is attempted to suppress by authority may possibly be true. Those who desire to suppress it, of course deny its truth; but they are not infallible. . . . To refuse a hearing to an opinion, because they are sure that it is false, is to assume that *their* certainty is the same thing as *absolute* certainty. All silencing of discussion is an assumption of infallibility. . . . while every one well knows himself to be fallible, few think it necessary to take any precautions against their own fallibility, or admit the supposition that any opinion, of which they feel very certain, may be one of the examples of the error to which they acknowledge themselves to be liable. Absolute princes, or others who are accustomed to unlimited deference, usually feel this complete confidence in their own opinions on nearly all subjects. People more happily situated, who sometimes hear their opinions disputed, and are not wholly unused to be set right when they are wrong, place the same unbounded reliance only on such of their opinions as are shared by all who surround them, or to whom they habitually defer: for in proportion to a man's want of confidence in his own solitary judgment, does he usually repose, with implicit trust, on the infallibility of "the world" in general. And the world, to each individual, means the part of it with which he comes in contact; his party, his sect, his church, his class of society. . . . it never troubles him that mere accident has decided which of these numerous worlds is the object of his reliance, and that the same causes which make him a Churchman in London, would have made him a Buddhist or a Confucian in Pekin. . . . The objection likely to be made to this argument would probably take some such form as the following. . . . Judgment is given to men that they may use it. Because it may be used erroneously, are men to be told that they ought not to use it at all? . . . If we were never to act on our opinions, because those opinions may be wrong, we should leave all our interests uncared for, and all our duties unperformed.

. . . Men, and governments, must act to the best of their ability. There is no such thing as absolute certainty, but there is assurance sufficient for the purposes of human life. We may, and must, assume our opinion to be true for the guidance of our own conduct: and it is assuming no more when we forbid bad men to pervert society by the propagation of opinions which we regard as false and pernicious.

I answer, that it is assuming very much more. There is the greatest difference between presuming an opinion to be true, because, with every opportunity for contesting it, it has not been refuted, and assuming its truth for the purpose of not permitting its refutation. . . . Why is it . . . that there is on the whole a preponderance among mankind of rational opinions and rational conduct? If there really is this preponderance—which there must be unless human affairs are, and have always been, in an almost desperate state—it is owing to a quality of the human mind, the source of everything respectable in man either as an intellectual or as a moral being, namely, that his errors are corrigible. He is capable of rectifying his mistakes, by discussion and experience. Not by experience alone. There must be discussion, to show how experience is to be interpreted. . . . The whole strength and value, then, of human judgment, depending on the one property, that it can be set right when it is wrong, reliance can be placed on it only when the means of setting it right are kept constantly at hand. In the case of any person whose judg-

ment is really deserving of confidence, how has it become
so? Because he has kept his mind open to criticism of his
opinions and conduct. Because it has been his practice
to listen to all that could be said against him. . . . the
only way in which a human being can make some approach to knowing the whole of a subject, is by hearing
what can be said about it by persons of every variety of
opinion, and studying all modes in which it can be looked
at by every character of mind. No wise man ever acquired
his wisdom in any mode but this; nor is it in the nature of
human intellect to become wise in any other manner.
. . . The most intolerant of churches, the Roman Catholic Church, even at the canonization of a saint, admits,
and listens patiently to, a "devil's advocate." The holiest
of men, it appears, cannot be admitted to posthumous
honors, until all that the devil could say against him is
known and weighed. . . .

The beliefs which we have most warrant for, have no
safeguard to rest on, but a standing invitation to the
whole world to prove them unfounded. . . . This is the
amount of certainty attainable by a fallible being, and this
the sole way of attaining it.

Strange it is, that men should admit the validity of the
arguments for free discussion, but object to their being
"pushed to an extreme"; not seeing that unless the reasons
are good for an extreme case, they are not good for any
case. . . . To call any proposition certain, while there is
any one who would deny its certainty if permitted, but
who is not permitted, is to assume that we ourselves, and
those who agree with us, are the judges of certainty, and
judges without hearing the other side.

Let us now pass to the second division of the argument.
. . . However unwillingly a person who has a strong
opinion may admit the possibility that his opinion may
be false, he ought to be moved by the consideration that
however true it may be, if it is not fully, frequently, and
fearlessly discussed, it will be held as a dead dogma, not
a living truth.

There is a class of persons . . . who think it enough
if a person assents undoubtingly to what they think true,

though he has no knowledge whatever of the grounds of the opinion, and could not make a tenable defense of it against the most superficial objections. Such persons, if they can once get their creed taught from authority, naturally think that no good, and some harm, comes of its being allowed to be questioned. . . . This is not knowing the truth. Truth, thus held, is but one superstition the more accidentally clinging to the words which enunciate a truth. . . . But, some one may say, "Let them be *taught* the grounds of their opinions. It does not follow that opinions must be merely parroted because they are never heard controverted." . . . such teaching suffices on a subject like mathematics, where there is nothing at all to be said on the wrong side of the question. . . . But when we turn to subjects infinitely more complicated, to morals, religion, politics, social relations, and the business of life, three-fourths of the arguments for every disputed opinion consist in dispelling the appearances which favor some opinion different from it. The greatest orator, save one, of antiquity, has left it on record that he always studied his adversary's case with as great, if not with still greater, intensity than even his own. What Cicero practiced as the means of forensic success, requires to be imitated by all who study any subject in order to arrive at the truth. He who knows only his own side of the case, knows little of that.

[*At this point Mill turns to deal with an argument that was made as recently as 1963 by the Deputy Attorney General of North Carolina, Ralph Moody, in defending that state's ban on Communist speakers: "It is a gross error to contend that colleges and universities are compelled by an overwhelming need to have members of the Communist Party come to the various campuses and talk to the students on the doctrines and principles of Communism. There are many patriotic and loyal professors in our institutions who are familiar with the theories expounded in Marx's book . . . who are familiar with Lenin's theories . . . and Trotsky's theories . . . and who are entirely competent to teach students about Communism. You do not have to talk to Communists to investigate their doc-*

trines and creeds."—*Excerpt from Memorandum to Attorney General of North Carolina in regard to the Constitutionality of Chapter 1207 of the Session Laws of 1963 (HB 1395) entitled: "An Act to Regulate Visiting Speakers at State Supported Colleges and Universities."*]

. . . Nor is it enough that he should hear the arguments of adversaries from his own teachers, presented as they state them, and accompanied by what they offer as refutations. That is not the way to do justice to the arguments, or bring them into real contact with his own mind. He must be able to hear them from persons who actually believe them; who defend them in earnest, and do their very utmost for them. He must know them in their most plausible and persuasive form; he must feel the whole force of the difficulty which the true view of the subject has to encounter and dispose of; else he will never really possess himself of the portion of truth which meets and removes that difficulty. Ninety-nine in a hundred of what are called educated men are in this condition; even of those who can argue fluently for their opinions. Their conclusion may be true, but it might be false for anything they know. . . . So essential is this discipline to a real understanding of moral and human subjects, that if opponents of all important truths do not exist, it is indispensable to imagine them, and supply them with the strongest arguments which the most skilful devil's advocate can conjure up.

To abate the force of these considerations, an enemy of free discussion may be supposed to say, that there is no necessity for mankind in general to know and understand all that can be said against or for their opinions by philosophers and theologians. That it is not needful for common men to be able to expose all the misstatements or fallacies of an ingenious opponent. That it is enough if there is always somebody capable of answering them. . . . The Catholic Church has its own way of dealing with this embarrassing problem. It makes a broad separation between those who can be permitted to receive its doctrines on conviction, and those who must accept them on trust. . . . thus giving to the *élite* more mental culture, though not more mental freedom, than it allows to the mass. By this device it succeeds in obtaining the kind of mental superiority which its purposes require; for though culture without freedom never made a large and liberal mind, it can make a clever *nisi prius* advocate of a cause. But . . . in the present state of the world, it is practically impossible that writings which are read by the instructed can be kept from the uninstructed. . . .

If, however, the mischievous operation of the absence of free discussion, when the received opinions are true, were confined to leaving men ignorant of the grounds of those opinions, it might be thought that this, if an intellectual, is no moral evil, and does not affect the worth of the opinions . . . The fact, however, is, that not only the grounds of the opinion are forgotten in the absence of discussion, but too often the meaning of the opinion itself. The words which convey it, cease to suggest ideas, or suggest only a small portion of those they were originally employed to communicate. Instead of a vivid conception and a living belief, there remain only a few phrases retained by rote; or, if any part, the shell and husk only of the meaning is retained, the finer essence being lost. The great chapter in human history which this fact occupies and fills, cannot be too earnestly studied and meditated on.

It is illustrated in the experience of almost all ethical doctrines and religious creeds. They are all full of meaning and vitality to those who originate them, and to the direct disciples of the originators. Their meaning continues to be felt in undiminished strength, and is perhaps brought out into even fuller consciousness, so long as the struggle lasts to give the doctrine or creed an ascendancy over other creeds. At last it either prevails, and becomes the general opinion, or its progress stops; it keeps possession of the ground it has gained, but ceases to spread further. When either of these results has become apparent, controversy on the subject flags, and gradually dies away. The doctrine has taken its place, if not as a received opinion, as one of the admitted sects or divisions of opinion: those who hold it have generally inherited, not adopted it. . . . From this time may usually be dated the decline in the living power of the doctrine. . . . manifesting its power by not suffering any fresh and living conviction to get in, but itself doing nothing for the mind or heart, except standing sentinel over them to keep them vacant.

. . . All languages and literatures are full of general observations on life, both as to what it is, and how to conduct oneself in it; observations which everybody knows, which everybody repeats, or hears with acquiescence, which are received as truisms, yet of which most people first truly learn the meaning, when experience, generally of a painful kind, has made it a reality to them. How often, when smarting under some unforeseen misfortune or disappointment, does a person call to mind some proverb or common saying, familiar to him all his life, the meaning of which, if he had ever before felt it as he does now, would have saved him from the calamity. There are indeed reasons for this, other than the absence of discussion: there are many truths of which the full meaning *cannot* be realized, until personal experience has brought it home. But much more of the meaning even of these would have been understood, and what was understood would have been far more deeply impressed on the mind, if the man had been accustomed to hear it argued *pro* and *con* by people who did understand it. The fatal tendency of mankind to leave off thinking about a thing when it is no longer doubtful, is the cause of half their errors. A contemporary author has well spoken of "the deep slumber of a decided opinion."

. . . If there are any persons who contest a received opinion, or who will do so if law or opinion will let them, let us thank them for it, open our minds to listen to them, and rejoice that there is some one to do for us what we otherwise ought, if we have any regard for either the certainty or the vitality of our convictions, to do with much greater labor for ourselves.

[*On February 20, 1964, George Lincoln Rockwell spoke on the campus of the University of Kansas. It was, in essence, Mill's second principle that the Chancellor of the university, Dr. W. Clark Wescoe, pronounced on that occasion in a statement distributed to the students: "I cannot recommend Rockwell to you. I despise his principles. I am convinced, however, that no one can be harmed by listening to him and that, conversely, his very presence may serve to make us all more dedicated to the principles of brotherhood as we come face to face with his repugnant views."]*

It still remains to speak of one of the principal causes which make diversity of opinion advantageous. . . . We have hitherto considered only two possibilities: that the received opinion may be false, and some other opinion, consequently, true; or that, the received opinion being true, a conflict with the opposite error is essential to a clear apprehension and deep feeling of its truth. But there is a commoner case than either of these; when the conflicting doctrines, instead of being one true and the other false, share the truth between them; and the nonconforming opinion is needed to supply the remainder of truth, of which the received doctrine embodies only a part. Popular opinions, on subjects not palpable to sense, are often true, but seldom or never the whole truth. . . . Heretical opinions, on the other hand, are generally some of these suppressed and neglected truths. . . . in the human mind, one-sidedness has always been the rule, and many-sidedness the exception. . . . Such being the partial character of prevailing opinions, even when resting on a true foundation, every opinion which embodies somewhat of the portion of truth which the common opinion omits, ought to be considered precious, with whatever amount of error and confusion that truth may be blended. . . .

Thus, in the eighteenth century, when nearly all the instructed, and all those of the uninstructed who were led by them, were lost in admiration of what is called civilization. . . . with what a salutary shock did the paradoxes of Rousseau explode like bombshells in the midst, dislocating the compact mass of one-sided opinion, and forcing its elements to recombine in a better form and with additional ingredients. Not that the current opinions were on the whole farther from the truth than Rousseau's were; on the contrary, they were nearer to it; they contained more of positive truth, and very much less of error. Nevertheless there lay in Rousseau's doctrine, and has floated down the stream of opinion along with it, a considerable amount of exactly those truths which the popular opinion wanted. . . .

In politics, again, it is almost a commonplace, that a party of order or stability, and a party of progress or reform, are both necessary elements of a healthy state of political life. . . . Unless opinions favorable to democracy and to aristocracy, to property and to equality, to co-operation and to competition, to luxury and to abstinence, to sociality and individuality, to liberty and discipline, and all the other standing antagonisms of practical life, are expressed with equal freedom, and enforced and defended with equal talent and energy, there is no chance of both elements obtaining their due; one scale is sure to go up, and the other down. Truth, in the great practical concerns of life, is so much a question of the reconciling and combining of opposites, that very few have minds sufficiently capacious and impartial to make the adjustment with an approach to correctness, and it has to be made by the rough process of a struggle between combatants fighting under hostile banners. . . . When there are persons to be found, who form an exception to the apparent unanimity of the world on any subject, even if the world is in the right, it is always probable that dissentients have something worth hearing to say for themselves, and that truth would lose something by their silence.

Mill's final point has been reiterated in another way by Professor Chafee.

Zechariah Chafee, Jr.: [5]

The effect of suppression extends far beyond the agitators actually put in jail, far beyond the pamphlets physi-

---

[5] Reprinted by permission of the publishers from Zechariah Chafee, Jr., *Free Speech in the United States* (Cambridge, Mass.: Harvard Uni-

cally destroyed. A favorite argument against free speech is that the men who are thus conspicuously silenced had little to say that was worth hearing. . . . my contention is that the pertinacious orators and writers who get hauled up are merely extremist spokesmen for a mass of more thoughtful and more retiring men and women, who share in varying degrees the same critical attitude toward prevailing policies and institutions. When you put the hotheads in jail, these cooler people do not get arrested— they just keep quiet. . . . Once the prosecutions begin, then the hush-hush begins too. Discussion becomes one-sided and artificial. Questions that need to be threshed out do not get threshed out.

These, then, are the arguments on behalf of freedom of speech. They are, indeed, the arguments for the democratic process itself, for as Justice Benjamin Cardozo once said, ". . . of freedom of thought and speech . . . one may say that it is the matrix, the indispensable condition, of nearly every other form of freedom." [6]

We have been concerned in this book primarily with what men may be permitted by law to say. How they choose to use their freedom is another matter. To Father Gardiner, and those who share his views, these questions may be identical, for as he put it, if a man knows the world is round and chooses to say it is flat he should not be allowed "to use his free will in that fantastic fashion." The libertarian, on the other hand, would take the position that one must be allowed to use his freedom of expression in any way he wishes, but that this does not prevent us from attempting to teach or persuade him to speak responsibly. Nor would we be precluded from urging his listeners to reject him if he does not.

There is no gainsaying the fact that many men abuse

versity Press), p. 561. Copyright, 1941, by the President and Fellows of Harvard College.

[6] *Palko* v. *Connecticut,* 302 US 319, 327 (1937).

*their freedom of speech, that audiences are often misled by
demagoguery and bad taste, and that this constitutes a
serious social problem.*[7] *But to the libertarian, the dangers
to our own freedom are too great and our knowledge of
good and bad too fallible to risk dealing with this problem
by coercion. We can, of course, warn speakers, as does Professor Chafee, that they make the defense of their liberty
more difficult by behaving irresponsibly.*

Zechariah Chafee, Jr.:[8]

This tendency toward suppression will be immensely
strengthened if speakers and writers use their privilege of
free discussion carelessly or maliciously, so as to further
their own ambitions or the immediate selfish interests
of their particular minority. By abusing liberty of speech,
they may further its abolition. I should be very slow to
lock such men up or confiscate their pamphlets, but I do
say that they owe it to the framers of the First Amendment . . . to think long and hard before they express
themselves, so as to be sure that they speak fruitfully. It is
hopeless for the law to draw the line between liberty and
license. Judges and juries cannot look into the heart of a
speaker or writer and tell whether his motives are patriotic
or mean. But the man can look into his own heart and
make that decision before he speaks out. Whatever efforts
of this sort unpopular persons make will do much to maintain the vitality of the First Amendment.

*Or, taking a somewhat less self-righteous view, we can
attempt, as Mill suggests, to be more tolerant and understanding.*

---

[7] Franklyn S. Haiman, "A Re-Examination of the Ethics of Persuasion," *Central States Speech Journal* (March, 1952), pp. 4-9, and "Democratic Ethics and the Hidden Persuaders," *Quarterly Journal of Speech*
(December, 1958), pp. 385-92.

[8] Reprinted by permission of the publishers from Zechariah Chafee,
Jr., *Free Speech in the United States* (Cambridge, Mass.: Harvard Uni-
versity Press), p. ix. Copyright, 1941, by the President and Fellows of
Harvard College.

John Stuart Mill:[9]

Before quitting the subject of freedom of opinion, it is fit to take some notice of those who say, that the free expression of all opinions should be permitted, on condition that the manner be temperate, and do not pass the bounds of fair discussion. Much might be said on the impossibility of fixing where these supposed bounds are to be placed; for if the test be offense to those whose opinion is attacked, I think experience testifies that this offense is given whenever the attack is telling and powerful, and that every opponent who pushes them hard, and whom they find it difficult to answer, appears to them, if he shows any strong feeling on the subject, an intemperate opponent. But this, though an important consideration in a practical point of view, merges in a more fundamental objection. Undoubtedly the manner of asserting an opinion, even though it be a true one, may be very objectionable, and may justly incur severe censure. But the principal offenses of the kind are such as it is mostly impossible, unless by accidental self-betrayal, to bring home to conviction. The gravest of them is, to argue sophistically, to suppress facts or arguments, to misstate the elements of the case, or misrepresent the opposite opinion. But all this, even to the most aggravated degree, is so continually done in perfect good faith, by persons who are not considered, and in many other respects may not deserve to be considered, ignorant or incompetent, that it is rarely possible on adequate grounds conscientiously to stamp the misrepresentation as morally culpable; and still less could law presume to interfere with this kind of controversial misconduct. With regard to what is commonly meant by intemperate discussion, namely invective, sarcasm, personality, and the like, the denunciation of these weapons would deserve more sympathy if it were ever proposed to interdict them equally to both sides; but it is only desired to restrain the employment of them against the prevailing

---

[9] From John Stuart Mill, "On Liberty," in Charles W. Eliot, ed., *The Harvard Classics* (P. F. Collier & Son, 1909), pp. 257-59.

opinion: against the unprevailing they may not only be used without general disapproval, but will be likely to obtain for him who uses them the praise of honest zeal and righteous indignation. Yet whatever mischief arises from their use, is greatest when they are employed against the comparatively defenseless; and whatever unfair advantage can be derived by any opinion from this mode of asserting it, accrues almost exclusively to received opinions. The worst offense of this kind which can be committed by a polemic, is to stigmatize those who hold the contrary opinion as bad and immoral men. To calumny of this sort, those who hold any unpopular opinion are peculiarly exposed, because they are in general few and uninfluential, and nobody but themselves feels much interested in seeing justice done them; but this weapon is, from the nature of the case, denied to those who attack a prevailing opinion: they can neither use it with safety to themselves, nor, if they could, would it do anything but recoil on their own cause. In general, opinions contrary to those commonly received can only obtain a hearing by studied moderation of language, and the most cautious avoidance of unnecessary offense, from which they hardly ever deviate even in a slight degree without losing ground: while unmeasured vituperation employed on the side of the prevailing opinion, really does deter people from professing contrary opinions, and from listening to those who profess them. For the interest, therefore, of truth and justice, it is far more important to restrain this employment of vituperative language than the other; and, for example, if it were necessary to choose, there would be much more need to discourage offensive attacks on infidelity, than on religion. It is, however, obvious that law and authority have no business with restraining either, while opinion ought, in every instance, to determine its verdict by the circumstances of the individual case; condemning every one, on whichever side of the argument he places himself, in whose mode of advocacy either want of candor, or malignity, bigotry, or intolerance of feeling manifest themselves; but not inferring these vices from the side which a person takes, though it be the contrary side of the question to our own: and giving merited honor to every one, whatever opinion he may hold, who has calmness to see and honesty to state what his opponents and their opinions really are, exaggerating nothing to their discredit, keeping nothing back which tells, or can be supposed to tell, in their favor. This is the real morality of public discussion: and if often violated, I am happy to think that there are many controversialists who to a great extent observe it, and a still greater number who conscientiously strive towards it.

CONCLUSION

Let us, to close, return once again to concrete cases, coming full circle back to the State of Illinois. The difference between admonitions to responsible speech and coercion became a key issue for the American Association of University Professors in 1960 when it was called upon to interpret the meaning of its statement of principles on academic freedom. The particular case in question was that of Leo Koch, a biology professor at the University of Illinois, who had written a letter published in the student newspaper condoning, under certain circumstances, the practice of premarital sexual intercourse. Koch was dismissed forthwith from the faculty.

The statement of principles that became a bone of contention within the academic community declares that although a professor, "when he speaks or writes as a citizen . . . should be free from institutional censorship or discipline," nevertheless, "he should at all times be accurate, should exercise appropriate restraint, should show respect for the opinion of others. . . ." There were many who felt that if a professor violates this standard, as Koch was charged with doing, he may justifiably be punished. But to others the statement was intended as an admonition, hopefully to be honored voluntarily, but never to be used as a basis for suppression.[10]

---

[10] "Academic Freedom and Tenure: The University of Illinois," *Bulletin of the American Association of University Professors* (March, 1963), pp. 25-43.

No one argued that Koch should, or could, be protected from unpopularity or any of the other powerful informal social sanctions that a community invokes against those whose views it dislikes. As Professor Warren Taylor wrote:

> All citizens, including professors, express their opinions publicly at their own peril. . . . Anyone who opens the windows of his mind cannot be too surprised if some throw stones.[11]

But informal social sanctions, overwhelming as they may be, differ in one significant respect from legal controls. They can, if one has the will and the courage, be ignored. The law cannot.

Four years after the Koch letter, another University of Illinois professor, Revilo P. Oliver, published an article in American Opinion, journal of the John Birch Society, commenting on the assassination of President John F. Kennedy in a way that made Leo Koch seem a master of self-restraint and a paragon of responsibility. The University, however, had learned from its four years of experience, and refrained this time from disciplinary action. The Board of Trustees, by an 8-1 vote, contented itself with a statement disassociating the university from Oliver's views.

Revilo P. Oliver thus remained a professor of classics at the University of Illinois, continuing to write prolifically and lecture vigorously on behalf of the radical right, and with each new exposure to public attention revealing more fully the lunacy of his political views. Leo Koch disappeared from the public scene. But the likelihood that his opinion about premarital intercourse has vanished with him is remote indeed.

Here once again we witness the futility of suppression and the value of liberty of expression. Leo Koch, regardless of his good judgment or lack of it, was addressing a problem that is vital to society and voicing a point of view that cannot be obliterated by prohibiting its expression. It can, to be sure, be driven underground and its propagation made difficult. But an idea never dies except by virtue of its own lack

---

[11] *Ibid.*, p. 42.

of merit, and it can become highly attractive, even without merit, if made taboo.

Revilo Oliver provides us with an opposite example. With confidence in the ultimate good judgment of our citizenry and in their ability to discriminate between sense and nonsense, we resist the temptation to curb his utterances. Allowed to speak freely, he eventually will be the executioner of his own ideas.

In this contrast of cases and their consequences may lie the essence of much that we know about freedom of speech.

QUESTIONS FOR DISCUSSION

1. On what basis might a Roman Catholic or anyone else who happened to believe in the existence of natural law still disagree fundamentally with Father Gardiner's point of view?

2. What, if any, validity is there to Berns' claim that the U. S. Supreme Court engages in the rendering of moral as well as legal judgments?

3. On the basis of Emerson's fourth argument, might not a shrewd dictator do well to allow complete freedom of speech? Are there other reasons why this would not be a practical policy for him to follow?

4. Does Mill provide a satisfactory answer to the argument of the Deputy Attorney General of North Carolina?

5. What, if any, real difference is there between an authoritative body (such as a university administration) admonishing persons under its jurisdiction to speak responsibly and its attempting to force them to do so?

Bibliography

"Academic Freedom and Tenure: The University of Illinois," *Bulletin of the American Association of University Professors* (March, 1963), 25-43.

Barth, Alan, *The Loyalty of Free Men* (New York: The Viking Press, 1951).

Berkowitz, Leonard, "The Effects of Observing Violence," *Scientific American* (February, 1964), 35-41.

Berns, Walter, *Freedom, Virtue and the First Amendment* (Baton Rouge: Louisiana State University Press, 1957).

Black, Hugo, "The Bill of Rights," 35 *New York University Law Review* 865 (1960).

Cahn, Edmond, "Justice Black and First Amendment Absolutes—A Public Interview," 37 *New York University Law Review* 549 (1962).

Cahn, Edmond (ed.), *The Great Rights* (New York: The Macmillan Company, 1963).

Castberg, Frede, *Freedom of Speech in the West* (Oslo, Norway: Oslo University Press, 1960).

Chafee, Zechariah, Jr., *Free Speech in the United States* (Cambridge, Mass.: Harvard University Press, 1948).

Chafee, Zechariah, Jr., book review of Alexander Meiklejohn, "Free Speech: And Its Relation to Self-Government," 62 *Harvard Law Review* 891 (1949).

Coons, John E., book review of Richard McKeon, Robert K. Merton, and Walter Gellhorn, "The Freedom to Read," 53 *Northwestern University Law Review* 127 (1958).

Cushman, Robert E., " 'Clear and Present Danger' in Free Speech Cases: A Study in Judicial Semantics," in Milton R. Konvitz (ed.), *Essays in Political Theory* (Ithaca, N.Y.: Cornell University Press, 1948), 311-24.

Downs, Robert B. (ed.), *The First Freedom* (Chicago: American Library Association, 1960).

Emerson, Thomas I., "Toward a General Theory of the

First Amendment," 72 *Yale Law Journal* 877 (1963).

Emerson, Thomas I. and David Haber, *Political and Civil Rights in the United States,* 2nd ed. (Buffalo, N.Y.: Dennis & Co., 1958).

Ernst, Morris L., *The First Freedom* (New York: The Macmillan Company, 1946).

Ernst, Morris L. and Alan U. Schwartz, *Censorship: The Search for the Obscene* (New York: The Macmillan Company, 1964).

Ernst, Morris L. and Alan U. Schwartz, *Privacy: The Right to Be Let Alone* (New York: The Macmillan Company, 1962).

Fraenkel, Osmond K., *The Supreme Court and Civil Liberties* (Dobbs Ferry: Oceana Publications, Inc., 1960).

Frantz, Laurent B., "The First Amendment in the Balance," 71 *Yale Law Journal* 1424 (1962).

Frantz, Laurent B., "Is the First Amendment Law?—A Reply to Professor Mendelson," 51 *California Law Review* 729 (1963).

Gardiner, Harold C., *Catholic Viewpoint on Censorship* (Garden City, N.Y.: Doubleday & Co., 1958).

Haiman, Franklyn S., "A Re-Examination of the Ethics of Persuasion," *Central States Speech Journal* (March, 1952), 4-9.

Haiman, Franklyn S., "Democratic Ethics and the Hidden Persuaders," *Quarterly Journal of Speech* (December, 1958), 385-92.

Hale, Swineburne, "The 'Force and Violence' Joker," *The New Republic* (January 21, 1920), 231-33.

Hook, Sidney, *Paradoxes of Freedom* (Berkeley: University of California Press, 1962).

Hudon, Edward G., *Freedom of Speech and Press* (Washington, D.C.: Public Affairs Press, 1963).

Hyman, Stanley Edgar, "In Defense of Pornography," *New Leader* (September 2, 1963), 13-15.

Jahoda, Marie, *The Impact of Literature: Psychological Discussion of Some Implications in the Censorship Debate* (New York: New York University Research Center for Human Relations, 1954).

Kalven, Harry, Jr., "The Metaphysics of the Law of Obscenity," *The Supreme Court Review,* 1960 (Chicago: University of Chicago Press), 1-45.

Kalven, Harry, Jr., "The New York Times Case: A Note on 'The Central Meaning of the First Amendment,' " *The Supreme Court Review,* 1964 (Chicago: University of Chicago Press), 191-221.

Kerr, Walter, *Criticism and Censorship* (St. Paul, Minn.: Bruce Publishing Co., 1956).

Konvitz, Milton R., *Bill of Rights Reader,* 2nd ed. (Ithaca, N.Y.: Cornell University Press, 1960).

Kronhausen, Eberhard and Phyllis Kronhausen, *Pornography and the Law* (New York: Ballantine Books, 1959).

Leflar, Robert A., "The Free-ness of Free Speech," 15 *Vanderbilt Law Review* 1073 (1962).

Levy, Leonard, *Legacy of Suppression* (Cambridge, Mass.: Harvard University Press, 1960).

Lockhart, William B. and Robert C. McClure, "Literature, the Law of Obscenity and the Constitution," 38 *Minnesota Law Review* 295 (1954).

Meiklejohn, Alexander, *Political Freedom* (New York: Harper and Brothers, 1960).

Mendelson, Wallace, "On the Meaning of the First Amendment," 50 *California Law Review* 821 (1962).

Mill, John Stuart, *On Liberty* (New York: Appleton-Century-Crofts, 1957).

Milton, John, *Areopagitica.*

Nathanson, Nathaniel, "The Communist Trial and the Clear-and-Present-Danger Test," 63 *Harvard Law Review* 1167 (1950).

Roche, John P., "The Curbing of the Militant Majority," *The Reporter* (July 18, 1963), 35-38.

Shaw, George Bernard, "Preface on the Censorship," in *The Shewing-Up of Blanco Posnet* (New York: Brentano's, 1913).

Stouffer, Samuel A., *Communism, Conformity and Civil Liberties* (Garden City, N.Y.: Doubleday & Company, 1955).

Sullivan, John Paul, "Editorials and Controversy: The

Broadcaster's Dilemma," 32 *The George Washington Law Review* 719 (1964).

Van Den Haag, Ernest, "Controlling Subversive Groups," *Annals of the American Academy of Political and Social Science* (July, 1955), 62-71.

Whipple, Leon, *Story of Civil Liberty in the United States* (New York: Vanguard Press, 1927).

Table of Cases

(Boldface type indicates primary reference to case)

Index